Fall into Math a

Writers

Robin Adair

Jill Ewing

Shirley Faircloth

Janice Nikoghosian

Cynthia Peterson

Darlene Smith

Sheila Wiebe

Editors

Sheryl Mercier

Nancy Norsworthy

Illustrator

Sheryl Mercier

FALL INTO MATH AND SCIENCE

This book contains materials developed by the AIMS Education Foundation. **AIMS** (**A**ctivities **I**ntegrating **M**athematics and **S**cience) began in 1981 with a grant from the National Science Foundation. The non-profit AIMS Education Foundation publishes hands-on instructional materials (books and the quarterly magazine) that integrate curricular disciplines such as mathematics, science, language arts, and social studies. The Foundation sponsors a national program of professional development through which educators may gain both an understanding of the AIMS philosophy and expertise in teaching by integrated, hands-on methods.

ISBN **978-1-881431-18-3**

Printed in the United States of America

Table of Contents

Index to Skills

MATH SKILLS

SCIENCE PROCESSES

I HEAR AND I FORGET

I SEE AND I REMEMBER

I DO AND I UNDERSTAND

—Chinese Proverb

Introduction

Many of the experiences in life seem to just "fall into place." We do not always plan these experiences, and sometimes we trip over them. This is especially true in elementary education when it comes to science. Unfortunately, many times we even "fall on our face" when approaching science.

This is not necessarily due to a lack of knowledge or a dislike of science; many times, it is due to a sense of being uncomfortable with the demands and vagueness of a science textbook. You are not only invited to fall into math and science, but to leap in, wallow around, and come out dripping with excitement!

The Project AIMS series for K-1 is based on seasons to make it convenient for you to incorporate these investigations into your present curriculum. Because of the peak learning experiences you will present to your students, they will be "falling all over themselves" to become involved.

This series is not designed with a specific scope and sequence, where each succeeding lesson is based on the preceding lessons. The investigations are written in such a way that your students will discover the true meaning of math and science integration—application of knowledge in the real world.

The Project AIMS K-1 series allows for flexibility for usage in your classroom. Use your own judgment to find the appropriate usage and development for each investigation.

Lest your principal and the parents of your students think you have "fallen off your rocker," and are no longer teaching math, each investigation has been provided with a student page to send home with your students.

This booklet is not intended to replace your science program, but is intended to be used as a supplement to the math-science curriculum. Remember that these experiments place prime emphasis on the science processes and skills. It is not necessary to have a laboratory and elaborate equipment to run a strong science program. All that is really needed is everyday materials and your willingness to try new ideas. GOOD LUCK!

—The K-1 Series Writing Team

Fall Into Math and Science

GRAPHING

Many of the investigations presented in the K-1 series of Project AIMS involve a variety of graphing activities.

Graphing is an invaluable technique that allows integration of many areas of the curriculum, which lends itself most readily to the integration of mathematics and science. It provides children with an opportunity to actively participate in problem solving experiences, from the concrete to the abstract.

The following mathematics skills are used in graphing:

attributes	ordinal numbers
counting	predicting
comparing (greater and fewer, more and less)	problem solving recording data
estimating	sets
interpreting data	sorting
logical thinking	tabulating
measuring	whole number computation
one-to-one correspondence	

The following science processes are used in graphing:

observing and classifying	gathering and recording data
measuring	interpreting data
estimating	applying and generalizing
controlling variables	

There are three types of graphs used in the investigations: real, representational and abstract.

Real graphs are the basis for building the concept of graphing. Students use manipulative objects with which to graph. They do not use drawing or other symbols. These graphs are usually done on a large area of floor or a table top.

Some examples of real graphs are:

1. People graph—students stand in boy and girl lines
2. Shoe graph—students take off shoes, place on floor next to appropriate word or picture (i.e. buckles, ties, boots)
3. Apple graph—students bring apples, graph by color

Some examples of real graphs found in this book are:

Apples A-Peel to Me
You Drive Me Crackers
Going Nuts

Representational graphs are the pictorial method of graphing. Students use pictures of the real object with which to graph. These graphs are usually placed on a wall or bulletin board.

Some examples of representational graphs are:

1. People graph—students draw pictures of themselves and place in appropriate line
2. Shoe graph—students draw pictures of own shoes and place under appropriate word or picture (see example above)
3. Apple graph—students draw pictures of own apple and place under matching color

Some examples of representational graphs found in this book are:

Boys and Girls
An Eyeful of Color
Don't Leaf Out the Vegetables

Abstract graphs are the symbolic method of graphing. Students use symbols with which to graph, instead of real objects or pictures. These graphs are also placed on a wall or bulletin board.

Some examples of abstract graphs are:

1. People graph—students use letter symbols to graph (i.e. B for boy and G for girl)
2. Shoe graph—students use different colored squares for graphing (i.e. red for buckles, yellow for ties, blue for boots)
3. Apple graph—students use different colored circles for graphing (i.e. red, green, yellow)

Some examples of abstract graphs found in this book are:

How Tall Are You?
Weather Wear
You Drive Me Crackers

Students need a great amount of experience with all three types of graphing. It is best if students move from real graphs through representational graphs and finally to abstract graphs. However, as they gain experience, this is not always necessary. Continue using all three types of graphs for maximum learning.

Suggested Graphing Questions

1. Which column has the least?

2. Which column has the most?

3. Are there more _____(reds)_____ or more _____(yellows)_____?

4. Are there less _____ or less _____?

5. How many _____ are there?

6. How many more _____ are there than _____?

7. How many less _____ are there than _____?

8. How many _____ are there altogether?

9. Are any columns the same?

10. Do more boys like _____ than girls?

11. Do more girls like _____ than boys?

• *Goal:* What can you tell me about the graph? Tell me a number sentence about the graph.

When children have had several experiences working with graphs, give them a turn at being "teacher."

Graphs

Real Graphs

Use real objects on a table or the floor.

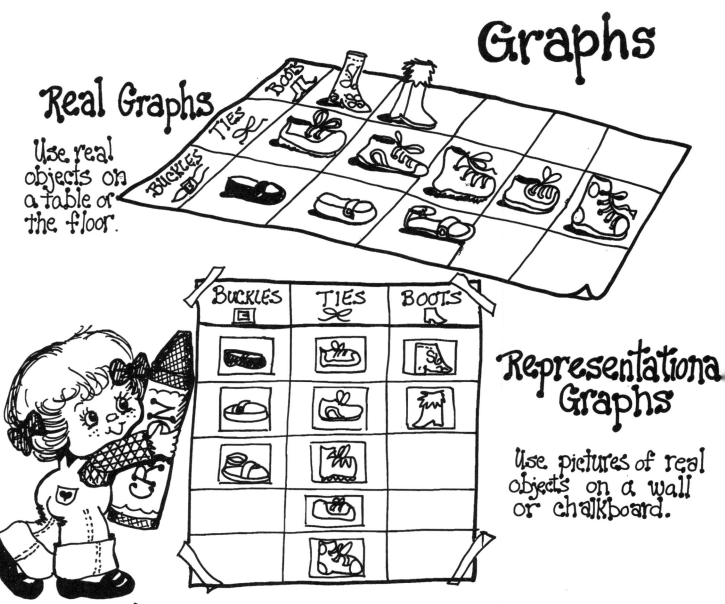

Representational Graphs

Use pictures of real objects on a wall or chalkboard.

Abstract Graphs

Use squares or circles of different colors to represent real objects. Usually place on a wall or chalkboard.

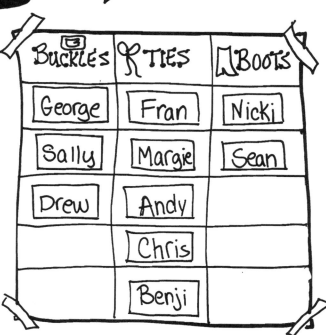

BUCKLES	TIES	BOOTS
George	Fran	Nicki
Sally	Margie	Sean
Drew	Andy	
	Chris	
	Benji	

You Can Count on Us

I. Topic Area
Class composition (boys/girls)

II. Introductory Statement
Students will discover whether there are more girls or more boys in their classroom.

III. Key Question
Are there more boys or more girls in our classroom?

IV. Math Skills
a. Predicting
b. Graphing
   1. Counting
   2. Equations

Science Processes
a. Gathering and recording data
b. Interpreting data
c. Applying and generalizing
d. Comparing

V. Materials
- Prediction cards—3″ × 4″ white construction paper, 1/child
- Boys/Girls Graph
- markers for the graph—4″ × 6″ tan construction paper, 1/child
- glue stick
- crayons
- pencils
- chalkboard
- chalk/eraser
- masking tape
- black marking pen

VI. Background Information
It is important to have *all* of the materials assembled prior to beginning this lesson.

VII. Management
1. This activity will take approximately 30-45 minutes.
2. This activity works best as a "whole class" activity.
3. The students should be seated at their desks where matrials (pencils and crayons) will be readily accessible.

VIII. Advanced Preparation
1. Mount the Boy/Girl Graph onto the chalkboard with masking tape. (Make sure that the students will be able to reach the graph.)
2. Place the chalk, eraser and glue stick near the graph.

IX. Procedure
1. Students predict whether there are more boys or girls in the classroom. On their white cards they will write:

 if they think there are more boys

 if they think there are more girls

(It's fun to tell the students that these white cards are "top secret" and that they are the only ones who will see their card.)
2. Students place their "secret" cards in a special place so as to keep them secret from other children in the class.
3. Each child draws a picture of himself/herself on a piece of tan paper. (drawings are done with crayons)
4. Students write their names either above or below their pictures using their pencils.
5. Students come to the graph and place their picture markers next to the appropriate word. (Boy, Girl)

X. Discussion
1. Did your secret card prove to be right?
2. Are there more girls or more boys in our classroom? (The children love to take out their secret cards and check to see if they were right!)
3. How many more boys/girls would we need to bring into our classroom in order to make both sets equal?
4. If we make another graph on a day when some of our boys or girls are absent, will our graph look any different than it does today? Why? Why not?

XI. Extensions
1. Compare your class graph to that of another class.
2. Do this graph (1/day) over a period of 3-5 days and watch to see how the results change due to absences.

XII. Curriculum Coordinates
Language Arts
1. "I Like Being a Boy/Girl Because..." Class Book
   —students draw themselves on a piece of 12″ × 18″ tan or white construction paper (Instruct the students to draw their pictures showing why they like being a boy or girl.)
   —words that complete the title sentence can be written onto each individual page by either the children or the teacher
   —house this class book in your classroom library
2. "I Like You" Game
   —the students make a picture of themselves (just like the picture used for the graph)
   —students fold their pictures and place them into a small paper bag
   —one child at a time steps forward and pulls out a card
   —the child must tell the rest of the class whose name he/she has drawn
   —the child who drew the name must look at the person whose name was drawn and say "I like you because..."
   —the child whose name was drawn proceeds to come forward and pulls out another card
   —this process continues until every child has had an opportunity to come forward

You Can Count on Us
Boy/Girl Graph

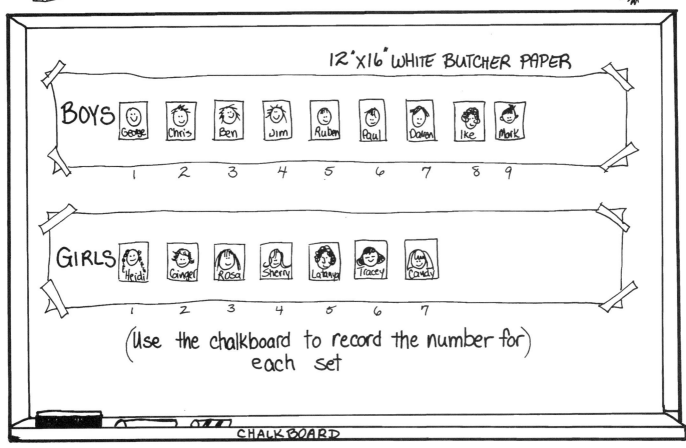

12"x16" WHITE BUTCHER PAPER

BOYS | George | Chris | Ben | Jim | Ruben | Paul | Darren | Ike | Mark

1   2   3   4   5   6   7   8   9

GIRLS | Heidi | Ginger | Rosa | Sherry | Latanya | Tracey | Candy

1   2   3   4   5   6   7

(Use the chalkboard to record the number for)
each set

CHALKBOARD

1. Mount the Boy/Girl Graph onto the chalkboard with masking tape. Place the chalk eraser and glue stick near the graphs
2. Students make their predictions and place them where they are not seen.
3. Each child draws a picture of himself/herself on a piece of tan 4"x6" construction paper. Students write their names above or below their picture.
4. Students come to the graph and place their picture markers next to the appropriate word (Boy, Girl).
5. When done, students take out their "secret" cards and check to see if they were right!

I like being a girl because:

4

An Eyefull of Color

I. Topic Area
The Human Body—Eyes

II. Introductory Statement
Students will discover which eye color is found most frequently among the boys and girls in their classroom.

III. Key Question
How could we find out which color of eyes is found more than any other color in our classroom?

IV. Math Skills
a. Predicting
b. Graphing
   1. Counting
   2. Equations

Science Processes
a. Gathering and recording data
b. Interpreting data
c. Applying and generalizing
d. Comparing

V. Materials
- Prediction Graph
- eye markers for Prediction Graph (x-blue, x-brown, x-green)*
- Eye Color Graph
- eye markers for Eye Color Graph (x-white with students names written on them)*
- glue stick
- small mirror
- * = the number of students in the classroom

VI. Background Information
The glue stick works very well to stick the eye markers to the graph. The graphs and eye markers *must* be assembled prior to beginning this activity.

VII. Management
1. This activity takes approximately 30 minutes.
2. This activity works best in a "total class" situation.
3. The children should be seated together in a small "cluster" so as to be more involved in this activity. (A carpeted "rest" or "library" area works well.)

VIII. Advanced Preparation
1. Place the Prediction and Eye Color Graphs in a place where the children will easily be able to see them.
2. Place the glue stick near the graphs.
3. Place the eye markers near the graphs where they will be easily accessible.

IX. Procedure
1. Students predict which eye color they think will be found most often in the classroom by placing an eye marker on the Prediction Graph under the eye that is colored the color that they think will be found most often.
2. Students take turns looking into the small mirror to find out what color their eyes really are.
3. Students place an eye marker with their name on it onto the Eye Color Graph under the correct color of their own eyes.

X. Discussion
1. Did the color that you thought we would find most often turn out to be the one that we did?
2. If we visited another classroom, would we find the same eye color more than any of the others? Why? Why not?
3. Would we find the same eye color to be the most common if we had looked at the girls' eyes? Boys' eyes?

XI. Extensions
1. Explore and discuss a model of an eye.
2. Draw and label the parts of the eye.
3. Compare your eye graph with that of another class.

XII. Curriculum Coordinates
Language Arts
1. "My Eyes Are the Same Color as..." Booklets.
Physical Education
1. The students can go on "sighted" (eyes open) walks and "non-sighted" (blindfolded) walks and then compare the two, stressing the important role that the eyes play in our everyday lives.

Prediction Graph

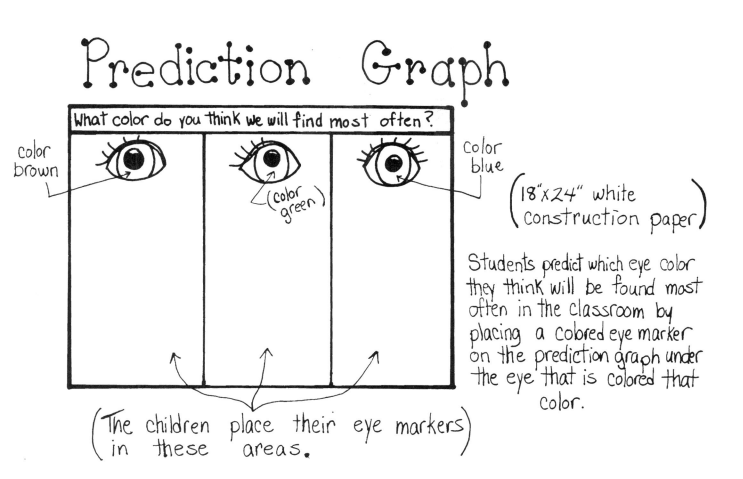

What color do you think we will find most often?

color brown

(color green)

color blue

(18"x24" white construction paper)

Students predict which eye color they think will be found most often in the classroom by placing a colored eye marker on the prediction graph under the eye that is colored that color.

(The children place their eye markers in these areas.)

Eye Color Graph

After the children predict what color is the most frequent, they take turns looking into the small mirror to find out what color their eyes are. They then place an eye marker (with their name on it) on to the eye color graph under the correct color.

Later, they may make their own eye color graph to match the class graph.

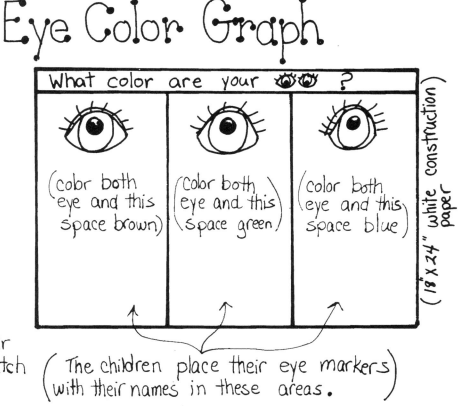

What color are your 👁👁 ?

(color both eye and this space brown)

(color both eye and this space green)

(color both eye and this space blue)

(18"x24" white construction paper)

(The children place their eye markers with their names in these areas.)

Eye Markers

Pattern

* For Prediction Graph:

    * Run on brown, blue, and green construction paper.

    * Run 1/child of each color so as to be sure to have enough.

* For Eye Color Graph:

    * Run on white construction paper.

    * Run 1/child.

    * Write names on these markers.

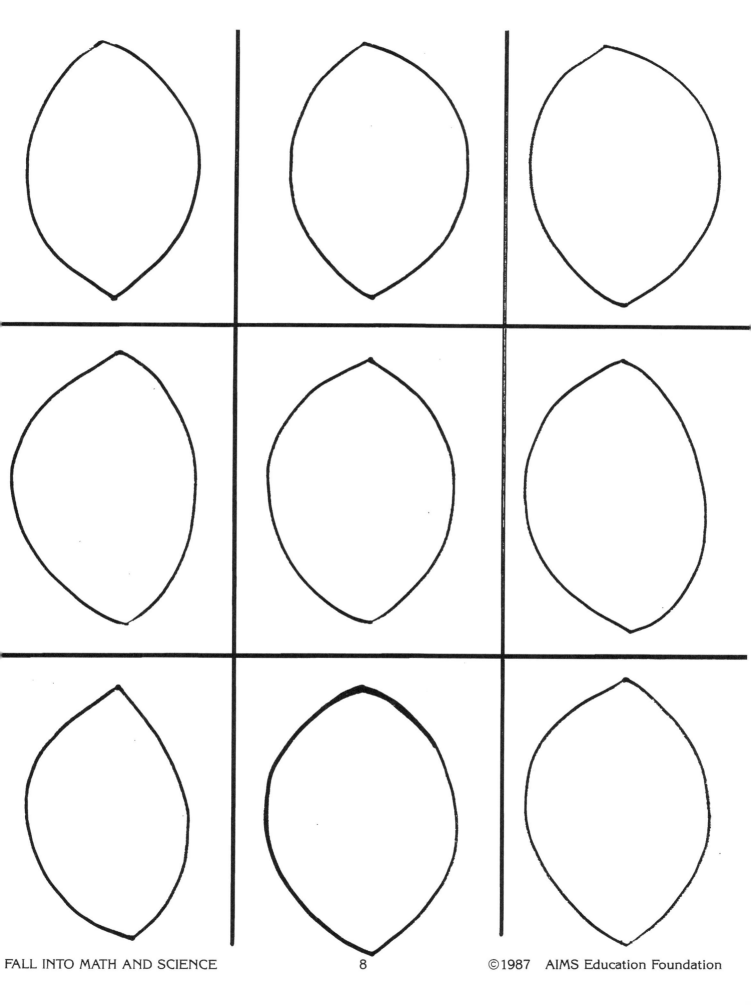

8

Eye Color Graph _____

brown	green	blue

The 👀 Have It

ART

Students color these eyes to match their own.

My are the same color as...

a bear

a tree

my hair

18"

12" Construction Paper

Fold the construction paper into fourths. Students will draw 3 pictures of things that are the same color as their eyes. Then they write the name of their picture either above or below their drawing.

 # How Tall Are You?

I. Topic Area
Human Growth

II. Introductory Statement
Students will learn how to determine their own height.

III. Key Question
How could we find out how tall we are? What would we need to do?

IV. Math Skills
a. Observing
b. Measuring (height)
c. Graphing
  1. Counting
  2. Equations
  3. Averaging
d. Logical thinking

Science Processes
a. Observing and classifying
b. Measuring
c. Gathering and recording data
d. Interpreting data
e. Applying and generalizing

V. Materials
- Measuring Graph
- name tags (1/child, each child's name is written on his/her name tag)
- masking tape
- glue stick

VI. Background Information
The children should be familiar with measuring in inches. The Measuring Graph and name tags *must* be constructed prior to beginning this lesson.

VII. Management
1. This activity takes approximately 30-45 minutes.
2. The children work in pairs during the measuring portion of this activity.

VIII. Advanced Preparation
1. Tape the Measuring Graph to the wall or the door.
2. Place the glue stick next to the graph.
3. Distribute the name tags to the children.

IX. Procedure
1. Students pick a partner to work with.
2. One pair of students at a time comes to the Measuring Graph. (the students bring their name tags with them)
3. One child stands in front of the graph. (the child's heels should be placed flat against the bottom of the Measuring Graph)
4. The partner takes the name tag of the child who is being measured, and places it on the graph at the line closest to where the top of his/her partner's head is touching.
5. Repeat steps 3 and 4 with the other partner being measured.
6. As one pair finishes measuring, another pair comes to the Measuring Graph. (Continue this process until every child has been measured.)

X. Discussion
1. How tall are you?
2. Who is the tallest person in our class?
3. Which numbers do we find the most students' names around?
4. Do you think that a graph done by another _____ grade (same grade) class would look about the same as ours? Why? Why not?
5. Do you think that a graph done by a _____ grade (higher or lower grade) class would look the same as ours? Why? Why not?

XI. Extensions
1. The children can take their height measurement in both feet and inches.
2. The children can take their height measurement using various "non-standard" units of measurement. (hands, pencils, crayons, books, etc.)
3. The children can compare their height at birth (approximately 20") with their present height.

XII. Curriculum Coordinates
Language Arts
1. The students can write "If I were as big as..." and/or "If I were as small as..." stories. (These stories can be assembled to make booklets that can be housed in the classroom library.)
2. Read *Inchworm* by Leo Lionni.
Art
1. The students can make their own "inchworm" rulers.

Measuring Graph

1. Make 6 copies of the inch worm graph on construction paper or tag. (use any color except black and green)

2. Use a flow pen or crayon, color the inch worms green.

3. Draw in the numbers with a black flow pen.

4. Glue the graph together- overlap at the dotted lines.

5. If you choose, this graph can be laminated and used over and over again.

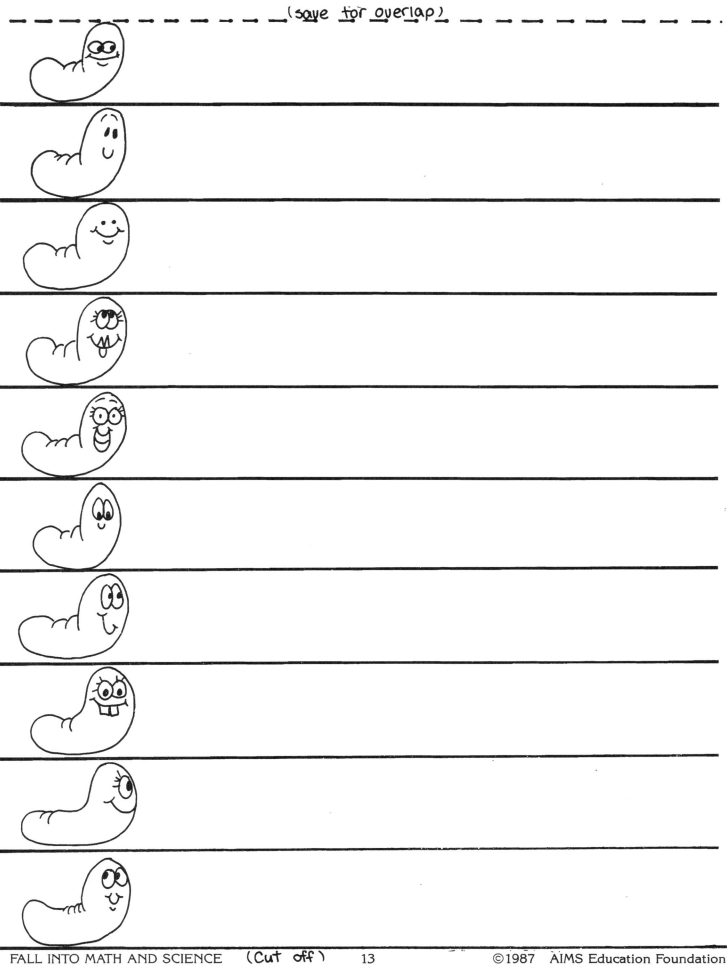

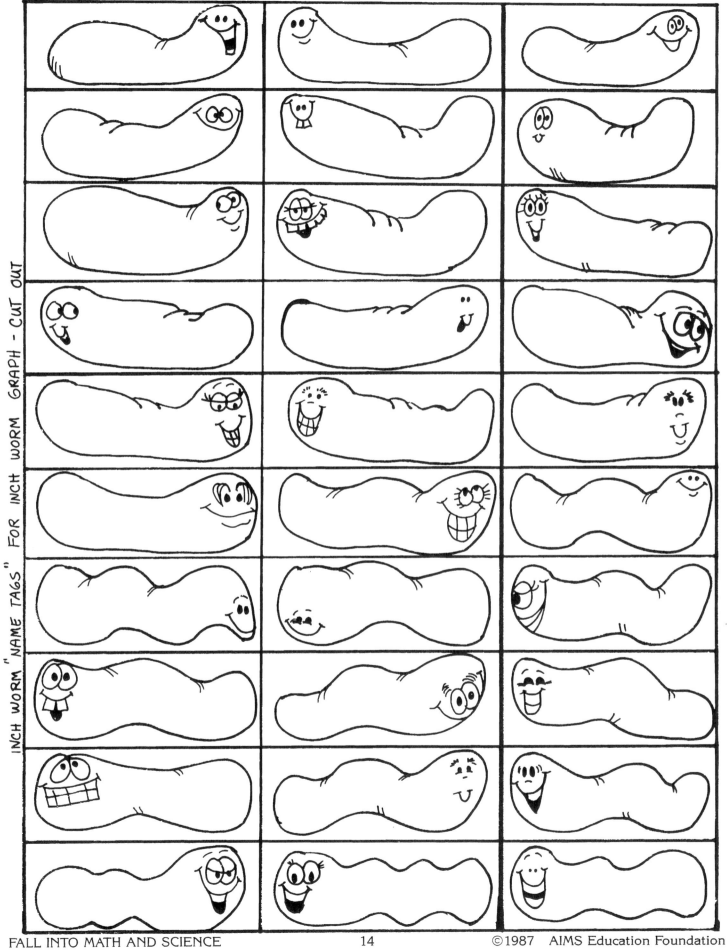

INCH WORM "NAME TAGS" FOR INCH WORM GRAPH – CUT OUT

name _____

Today, I am

_____ inches
tall.

_____
teacher

name _____

Today, I am

_____ inches
tall.

_____
teacher

name _____

Today, I am

_____ inches
tall.

_____
teacher

name _____

Today, I am

_____ inches
tall.

_____
teacher

Inchworm Rulers

Teacher... Run pattern on light colored construction paper (any color except black or green).

Students: 1. Color the inchworms green.

2. Use a black crayon to write the numbers for the inches on the ruler in the same manner as was used on the class measuring graph.

3. Cut out the rulers. Overlap and paste to the dotted line.

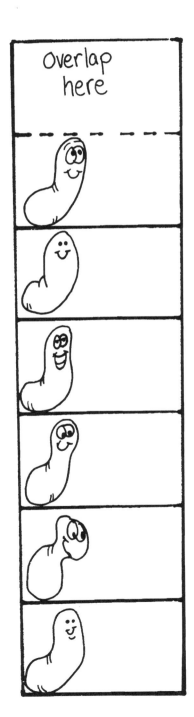

overlap here

overlap   overlap   overlap

Inchworm
Tape
Measure

Print on light colored
construction paper.
Cut out & piece
together with
tape.

A Weigh We Go

I. Topic Area
Human growth (weight)

II. Introductory Statement
Each student will discover his/her own weight.

III. Key Question
How much do you weigh?

IV. Math Skills

Math Skills
a. Sequencing/Ordinality
b. Graphing
   1. Predicting
   2. Comparing
   3. Counting
   4. Equations (difference)
c. Measuring (weighing)

Science Processes
a. Gathering and recording data
b. Interpreting data
c. Applying and generalizing
d. Measuring

V. Materials
- bathroom scale
- pencils (1/student)
- crayons (1 red and 1 green/student)
- slips of scratch paper for recording weight at scale (1 slip/student)
- student sheet (1/student)

VI. Background Information
1. It is helpful to have a number line or number chart that shows the numbers 1-100 clearly visible to the students throughout this activity.
2. Ask the students to color very lightly with their crayons so that they will still be able to see the numbers on their graphs.

VII. Management
1. This activity takes 60-90 minutes.
2. This activity can be conducted in either a total class or small group situation.
3. If this activity is done with the total class, students come in small groups to be weighed.

VIII. Advanced Preparation
1. Place the scale and slips of scratch paper at a station.
2. "Work-through" an entire student sheet with the students seated close enough to you to really see what is going to be expected of them. (Choose one student as an example and fill-out the student sheet appropriately—see numeral IX to find the steps.)

IX. Procedure
1. Students fill-in the boxes on the graph by writing the numbers 1-100.
2. Students predict how much they will weigh and color that number red on their graphs.
3. Students write the number of their prediction on the blank line by #1 at the bottom of their sheets.
4. Students come to the weighing station. As the child is weighed, he/she writes his/her weight on a slip of paper to take back to his/her desk.
5. Students find the number that shows how much they actually weigh and color it green on the graph.
6. Students write their actual weight on the blank line by #2 at the bottom of their sheets.
7. Students are asked by the teacher to look at their green number and their red number, and then asked to circle the smaller number with their pencils.
8. The students are asked by the teacher to put their finger on the number that comes after their circled number.
9. Students are instructed by the teacher to begin counting with "1" (the number where their finger is pointing) and count all of the boxes up to and including the next colored box.
10. Students write the number of boxes that they counted on the blank line by #3 at the bottom of their sheets.

X. Discussion
1. Did you weigh what you predicted you would?
2. Did you weigh more or less than you thought you would?
3. Do you think that you weigh more now, or when you were a baby? Why?
4. What do you think will happen to your weight as you get older?
5. Do you think that all first graders weigh the same? How could we find out for sure?

XI. Extensions
1. Students plot their actual weights on a class graph.
2. Students compare their own weight to that of another student in the class.
3. Students can determine how many pounds they have gained since birth.

XII. Curriculum Coordinates
Language Arts
1. "Stand-up" Booklets (see the following page for instructions)

_____
- - - - - - - - - - - - -
_____
Name

I weigh

_____ pounds

today.

_____
teacher

_____
- - - - - - - - - - - - -
_____
Name _____

I weigh

_____ pounds

today.

_____
teacher

_____
- - - - - - - - - - - - -
_____
Name

I weigh

_____ pounds

today.

_____
teacher

_____
- - - - - - - - - - - - -
_____
Name _____

I weigh

_____ pounds

today.

_____
teacher

A Weigh We Go ...
STAND - UP - BOOKLET

ART & LANGUAGE IDEA

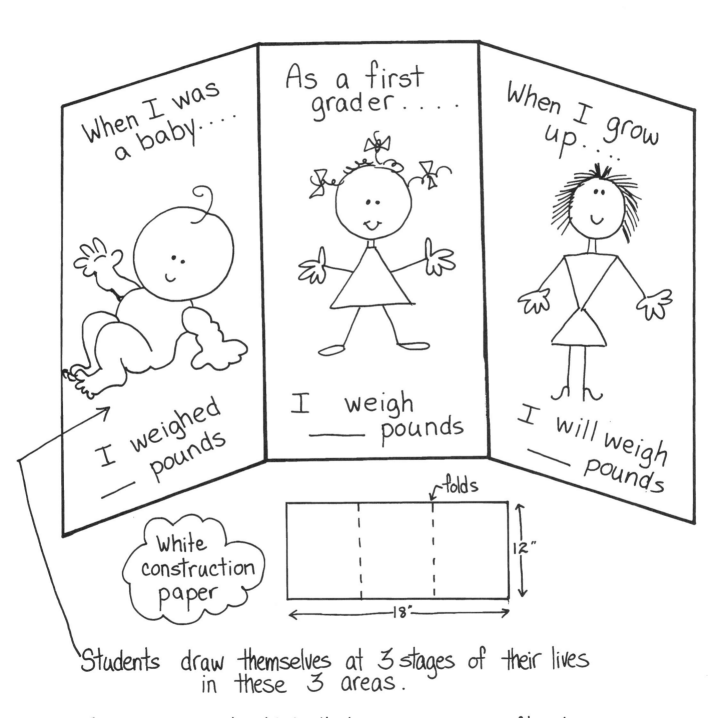

When I was a baby....

I weighed ___ pounds

As a first grader....

I weigh ___ pounds

When I grow up....

I will weigh ___ pounds

White construction paper

folds

12"

18"

Students draw themselves at 3 stages of their lives in these 3 areas.

This makes a booklet that is a super gift idea. It can be "stood-up" on a desk or table.

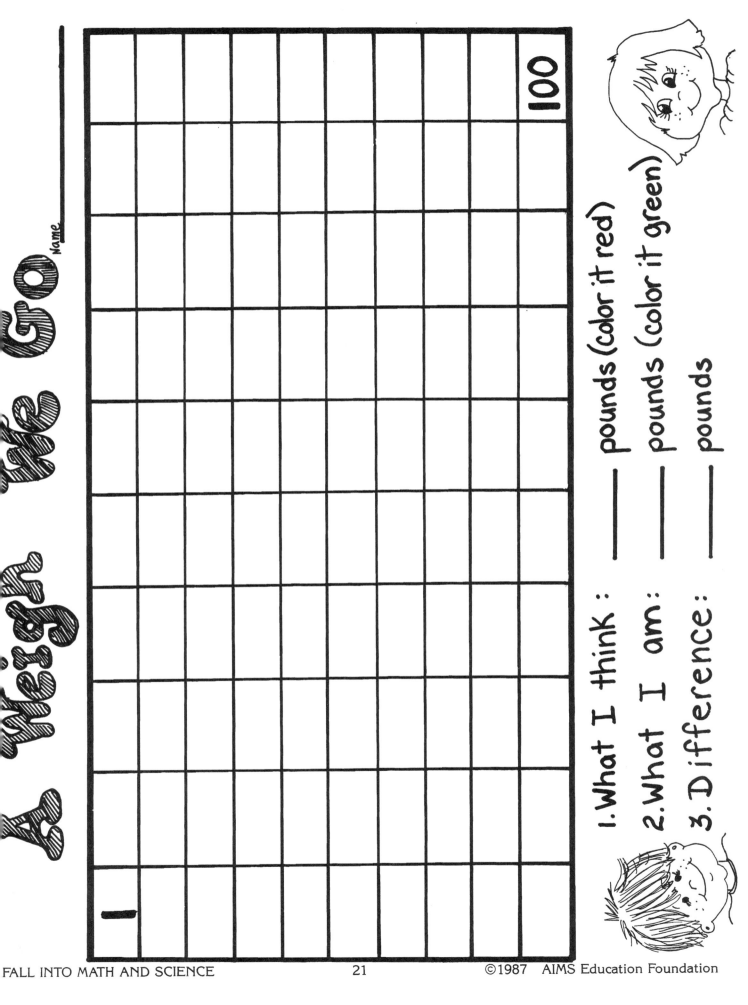

A Weigh We Go

Name

100

1. What I think : _____ pounds (color it red)

2. What I am : _____ pounds (color it green)

3. Difference : _____ pounds

I. Topic Area
Weather

II. Introductory Statement
Students will learn that weather influences what they wear.

III. Key Questions
What are you wearing today? What is the weather like today?

IV. Math Skills
a. Graphing
1. Counting
2. Whole number computation
3. Interpreting data

Science Processes
a. Observing and classifying
b. Gathering and recording data
c. Interpreting data
d. Applying and generalizing

V. Materials
- Graph
- Paper markers or xeroxed photos for graph (4 for each child)

VI. Background Information
Students need to have some understanding of words used for describing weather, such as sunny, foggy, overcast, cold, etc.

You may want to change some of the categories listed on the graph to fit the climate in your area.

VII. Management
1. This activity takes about 20-30 minutes.
2. It can be done with the whole class or in small groups.

VIII. Advanced Preparation
1. Prepare the graph. Suggested format (24" × 36"):
2. Cut markers to fit graph (approximately 1" × 1"). Make 4 markers for each child. Use one color for the boys' markers and a different color for the girls', or use xeroxed copies of students' photos for the markers.

Suggested format 24" x 36"

weather	What Are You Wearing Today?	date
pants and shirt		
shorts and shirt		
dress or skirt and blouse		
shoes		
sandals		
sweater		
jacket or coat		

IX. Procedure

1. Discuss each of the categories shown on the graph. For example, the first column might mean "jeans and a T-shirt" and also mean "a blouse and slacks". Have the students think about which categories apply to them.

2. Go through the categories again and have the students place their markers on the graph.

3. Discuss the graph.
   —Which column has the most? Why?
   —Which column has the fewest? Why?
   —Is there a column that doesn't have any markers? Why?
   —Is there a column that has only boys' markers? Only girls'?
   —Find the combined total for columns 1, 2, and 3.
   —Find the combined total for columns 4 and 5. Is it the same as the total for the first three? Why or why not?

4. Ask the class the date and record it on the graph.

5. Have the students describe the weather and record it on the graph. Discuss how the weather may have influenced the type of clothing they are wearing.

X. Discussion

1. What is the weather like today?
2. How does the weather influence what we wear?
3. What are some other factors besides weather that influence what we wear?
4. If we did this graph again next week (or next month, in January, at Thanksgiving) would it look the same? Which categories might be the same? Different?

XI. Extensions

1. Save the graph and then do the same activity at a different time of the year. Compare graphs.

2. Do this activity at the beginning of each season and compare.

3. Try covering the weather section of a graph done earlier in the year and see if the class can determine, by using the information on the graph, what the weather was like on that day.

XII. Curriculum Coordinates

Language Arts

1. Read Aesop's fable "The Wind and the Sun".
2. Read Dick Bruna's book, *My Shirt is White.*
3. Have the children think of clothing that would be appropriate for different types of weather (mittens, sundress, raincoat, for example). List these words on charts for experience stories or on word cards for categorizing activities.

Music

1. Hap Palmer's song "What Are You Wearing" (*Learning Basic Skills Through Music,* Vol. I)
2. Songs about the weather.

Social Studies

1. Find out how people of other cultures dress for weather similar to the weather in your area.

What are you wearing today?

_____ Name

Please draw in my face, my hair, and my clothes so that I will look just like you do today.

Today, the weather is

_____

Apples A Peel To Me

I. Topic Area
Apples

II. Introductory Statement
Students will learn about the different varieties of apples.

III. Key Question
How many different words can we use to describe an apple?

IV. Math Skills
a. Graphing
1. Whole number computation
2. Solving simple equations
3. Using a formula
4. Ordinal numbers
5. Predicting
b. Fractional numbers
c. Equations
d. Geometry
e. Sorting

Science Processes
a. Observing and classifying
b. Comparing
c. Applying and generalizing
d. Controlling variables
e. Gathering and recording data
f. Interpreting data
g. Measuring

V. Materials
- Red, green, and yellow apples—a different number of each color allows variance on the graph (if extension activities are to be used, allow one of each color apple for every four students; the applesauce recipe will require an additional eight apples)
- Posterboard and marking pens for graph (see advanced preparation)
- One student graph per child (provided for duplication)
- Red, green, and yellow crayons—one of each color per child

VI. Background Information
The different varieties of apples are readily available in late September to early November.

VII. Management
1. This activity works well in a whole class situation with teacher supervision.
2. The discussion and graphing activities will take approximately 30-45 minutes.

VIII. Advanced Preparation
1. Purchase apples.
2. Prepare classroom graph.
3. Duplicate and distribute student graph and crayons.

IX. Procedure
1. The teacher asks the key question, "What words can be used to describe an apple?" The teacher lists these describing words on chart paper or the chalkboard to be used in later language extension activity.
2. The students count the apples as the teacher removes them from a bag.
3. The teacher asks the students how the apples could be sorted into different groups based on the types of describing words they used in Step 1 (size, shape, color). The apples are then sorted by selected students into three color groups.
4. Have the entire class count the number of apples in each color group. Color in one box in the corresponding colored column of the class graph. Have the children duplicate this procedure on their individual graphs until all the apples in the red color group have been graphed. Repeat this procedure for each remaining color group.
5. Discuss the graph.

X. Discussion
1. What is different about all these apples? What is similar?
2. What kinds of things about apples can we learn from reading our class graph? What things will our graph not tell us? How could we answer these questions?
3. What types of other activities could we do with apples?

XI. Extensions
1. Graphing ideas:
   a. Have a taste test and graph each child's preference.
   b. Peel, core, and slice different varieties of apples so children do not know the color. Have the children taste the apples and graph their color prediction.
2. Make applesauce in small groups.

   Applesauce

   8 medium cooking apples—cut into fourths
   ½ cup water
   ½ cup packed brown sugar
   ¼ teaspoon ground cinnamon
   ¼ teaspoon ground nutmeg

   Heat apples and water to boiling over medium heat; reduce heat. Simmer uncovered, 5 to 10 minutes. Stir in remaining ingredients. Heat to boiling and stir 1 minute.

   Can be served in paper cups with a spoon or on graham crackers.

XII. Curriculum Coordinates

Language Arts

1. Make an apple book using the student's describing words from the chalkboard. The student's page could be duplicated from the apple pattern provided.

2. Read books and discuss the life of Johnny Appleseed.

Physical Education

1. Place the children into relay teams of 8-10 members. Give each captain an apple and place it under his/her chin. Have each team pass the apple down his or her team line, from chin to chin, using no hands.

2. Bob for apples in a tub of water.

Art

1. Make apple prints. Cut apples in half and place cut side down in pans of autumn colored tempera paint. Press the apple onto white construction paper to create an apple print.

Apples A Peel To Me

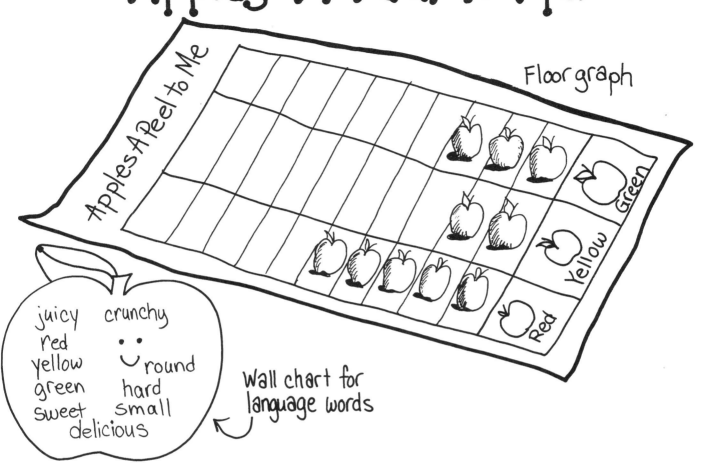

Floor graph

Apples A Peel to Me

Green
Yellow
Red

juicy   crunchy
red
yellow
green   hard
sweet   small
delicious
round

Wall chart for
language words

Ask the students how the apples could be sorted according to their describing words. Then have selected students sort them into 3 color groups. Have the entire class count the number of apples in each color group as you place them on the floor graph. As you remove each red apple, color in the box it was in. Have the students duplicate this process on their individual graphs. Repeat this process for each remaining color group. Discuss the graph.

For a representational graph, use the page of apple faces for a taste test graph. Have each student pick the color of the apple that they prefer, put their name on the apple and glue to a wall graph or the chalkboard.

I ♥ 🍎

Red   Yellow   Green

Apples A Peel to

Name _____

Red	Yellow	Green

Apple Art
The Apple Tree Cycle

Make a large apple shaped chart with these instructions ⟶

You will need:

* 12"x18" construction
* 4"x1" brown construction for tree trunks (4 per child)
* brown crayon
* pink, green, red, orange, & yellow tempera paint
* carrot slices
* sponge pieces for each color of paint

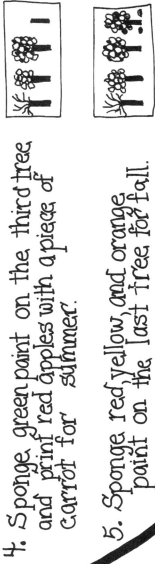

1. Glue 4 pieces of brown paper on your paper to make tree trunks.

2. Use a brown crayon and draw branches on the first tree for winter!

3. Sponge pink paint on the second tree for spring.

4. Sponge green paint on the third tree and print red apples with a piece of carrot for summer.

5. Sponge red, yellow, and orange paint on the last tree for fall.

That is my Life Cycle

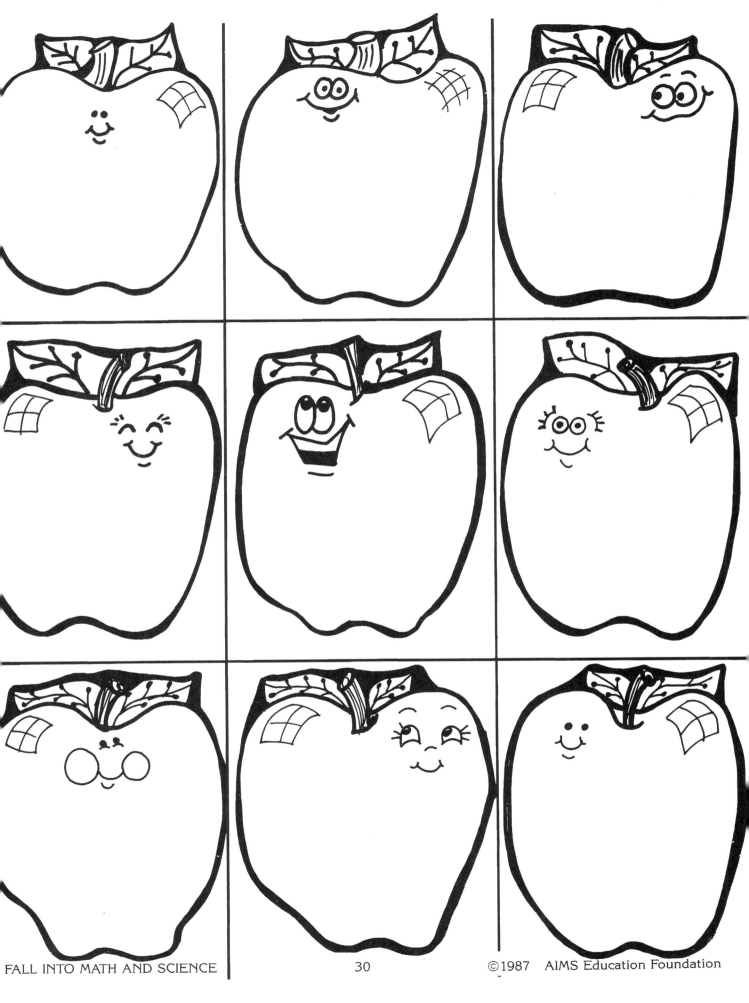

30

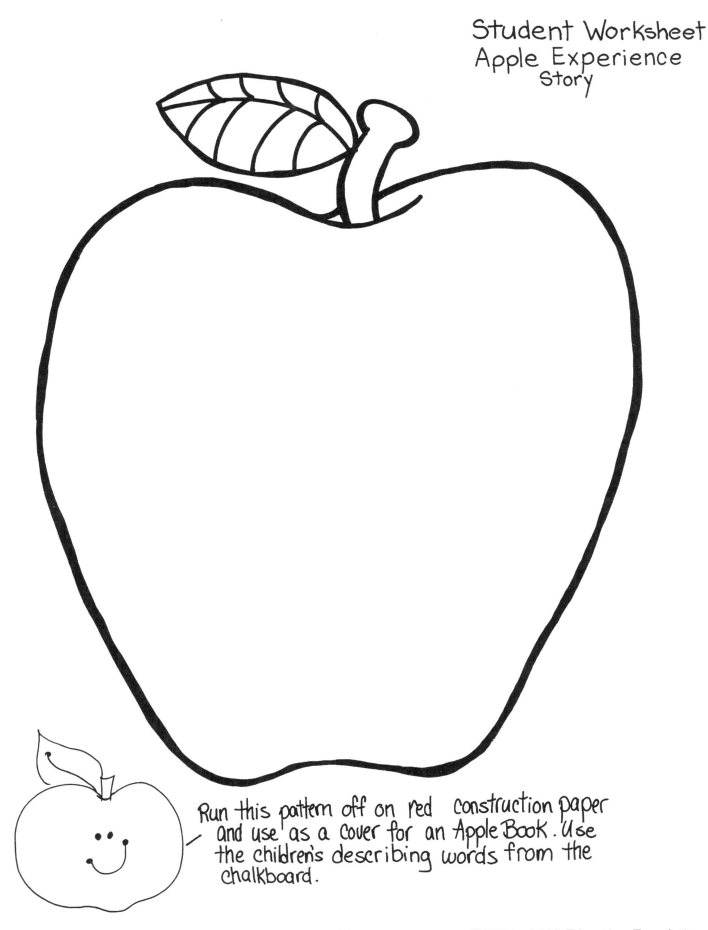

Run this pattern off on red construction paper and use as a cover for an Apple Book. Use the children's describing words from the chalkboard.

This certificate is to guarantee that

_____ is a

Good

_____ _____
Teacher   Date

Grapes to Raisins

I. Topic Area
Food

II. Introductory Statement
The students will learn that raisins come from grapes.

III. Key Question
What do you think would happen to grapes if they were left out in the sun for several days?

IV. Math Skills
a. Counting
b. Estimating
c. Observing
d. Recording data
e. Sorting

Science Processes
a. Observing
b. Estimating
c. Gathering and recording data
d. Interpreting data

V. Materials
- Thompson Seedless grapes (about 3 pounds)
- Chart paper for recording daily observations
- A cardboard box (the sides should be about 2 inches high)

VI. Background Information
Thompson Seedless grapes are usually available from June to November. Grapes dry fastest in hot, dry weather, so the best time to do this investigation is in September or in early October. It may take up to 3 weeks or more for all the grapes to turn into raisins.

If the weather is not conducive to drying grapes outside, you can dry them in an oven or toaster oven. It takes approximately 24 hours for grapes to dry in the oven. Set oven temperature to "warm". A food dehydrator can also be used in place of an oven.

VII. Management
1. Allow about 30 minutes for the first and last lesson.
2. Allow 5 to 10 minutes each day for discussing changes and recording observations.

VIII. Advanced Preparation
1. Have grapes ready.
2. Prepare chart for recording observations. Suggested format:

Day or Date	Observations

IX. Procedure
1. Show the grapes to the class. Talk about where the grapes came from, how they grow, etc. Have the students describe how the grapes look, feel, taste, and smell. (You may want to record these descriptions to refer to at a later time.)
2. Ask the key question: "What do you think would happen to grapes if they were left out in the sun for several days?"
3. Put the grapes in the box and put the box outside in direct sunlight or in a sunny spot by a window.
4. Each day ask the children if they have noticed any changes in the grapes. Record this information on the daily observations chart. Be sure to list "no change" if none is observed.
5. After some of the grapes have changed color, you may want to have the children sort the grapes by color. Record the results.
6. When all the grapes have turned into raisins, have the students discuss what they found out about grapes and raisins.

X. Discussion
1. What effect did the sun have on the grapes? Why?
2. How long did it take for all of the grapes to turn into raisins?
3. Did all of the grapes change at the same time?
4. How is a raisin like a grape? How is it different?

XI. Extensions
1. Try the above activity using a different variety of grape.
2. Investigate the effects of the sun on other foods or on non-food items.

XII. Curriculum Coordinates
Language Arts
1. Have the students recall the steps for changing grapes to raisins. Record these on a chart for a language experience story.
2. Read Aesop's fable "The Fox and the Grapes."
3. Make two charts; one in the shape of a grape, and the other in the shape of a raisin. Ask the students to think of words that describe grapes and raisins. Record these words on the appropriate chart.

Physical Education
1. For a creative movement activity, have the students show how a grape shrivels into a raisin.

Social Studies
1. Trace the journey of a raisin from the vine to the grocery shelf.

Grapes to Raisins

Language Development

Make 2 wall charts...

...One in the shape and color of a grape

12"x18" construction paper

juicy sweet round green

wet delicious

...One in the shape and color of a raisin

shriveled sweet chewy wrinkled

On each chart, write the children's words to describe grapes and raisins.

When the experiment is over, have the children describe all the steps of 'grapes to raisins'. Record the steps on a chart for display.

Grapes to Raisins

1. We put the grapes in the sun.
2. They started to turn brown.
3. We waited for 37 days.
4. The grapes shriveled to raisins.
5. We ate them!

(Sample Steps)

1. We put the grapes in the sun.

2. They started to turn brown.

3. We waited for   days.

4. The grapes shriveled to raisins.

5. We ate them!

(Your chart will vary with your own experience.)

Make copies of their story on the blank Grapes to Raisins page for students to take home.

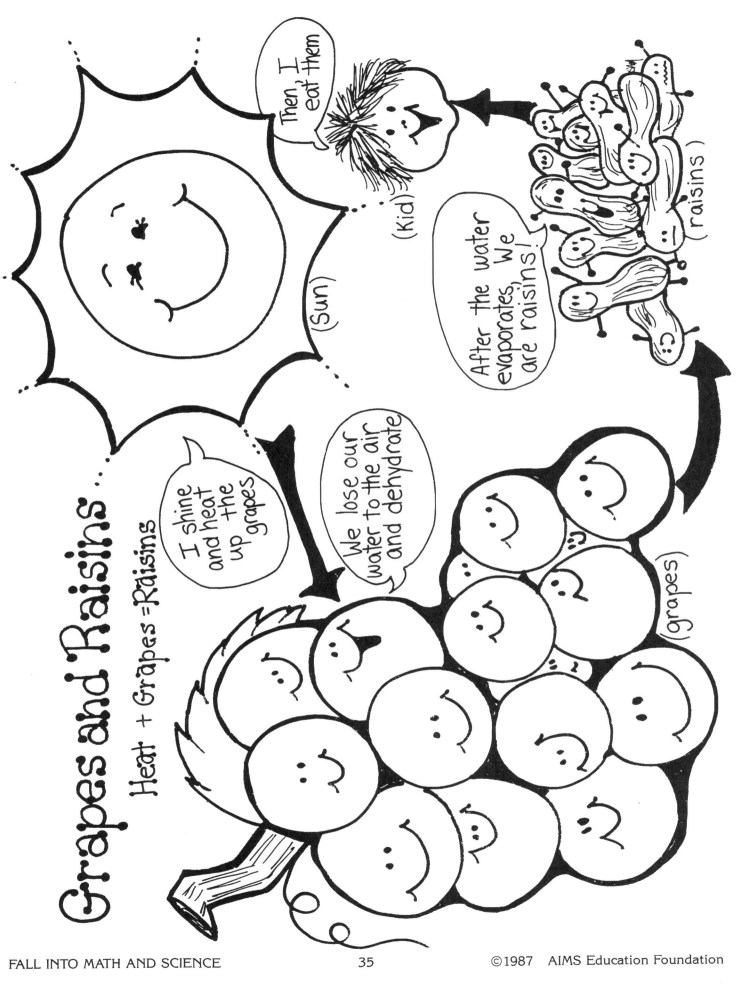

FALL INTO MATH AND SCIENCE   35   ©1987   AIMS Education Foundation

Grapes to Raisins

Fall Leafs Me Happy

I. Topic Area
Plant Life

II. Introductory Statement
Students will explore the many facets of leaves.

III. Key Question
What can we find out about these leaves?

IV. Math Skills
a. Attributes
b. Counting
c. Generalizing
d. Interpreting data
e. Measuring length
f. Observing
g. Patterns
h. Recording data

Science Processes
a. Observing and classifying
b. Measuring
c. Gathering and recording data
d. Interpreting data
e. Applying and generalizing

V. Materials
- Leaves collected by students
- Poster board
- Student page
- Rulers (one for each child)
- Magnifying lenses (one for each child)

VI. Background Information
1. The leaves will dry out and crumble if left too long. Investigation should be completed within a few days after students bring in leaves.
2. Students should have previous experience with rulers before working on this investigation.

VII. Management
1. This activity works best with small groups (not more than seven in a group).
2. This activity will take 30 to 45 minutes.

VIII. Advanced Preparation
1. Ask students to bring 2-3 leaves each from home or the playground. Instruct the students to pick up leaves from the ground and not from off a tree.
2. As children bring in leaves, glue or tape them on a poster board to create interest and easy display.
3. Duplicate student page (at end of investigation).
4. Be certain to have rulers and magnifying lenses ready for use.

IX. Procedure
1. Point out "leaf board" to students. Ask the Key Question—"What can we find out about these leaves?"
2. Allow students to share ideas about what they can find out about the leaves. (See X. **Discussion**) After students have discovered color, shape, length, pattern, etc., tell them they are going to measure the leaves to see them up close.
3. Instruct students on the proper use of a magnifying lens.
4. Guide students as they look at the leaf through the lens. Point out and discuss the veins, the colors, and the way the size of the leaf seemed to change.
5. Remind students of the proper use of a ruler.
6. Hand out rulers and student page.
7. Assist students in measuring at least four leaves. Let the students decide whether they want to measure length, width, etc.
8. The students should record these measurements on the student page.
9. After all measurements have been recorded, ask the students to share the length of their longest or shortest leaf.
10. Have the children pick up their magnifying lenses and ask them to look at their favorite leaf on the "leaf board."
11. Ask them to draw a picture, on the student page, of what the leaf looked like through the lens.
12. You may want to display these on the bulletin board for future discussion.

X. Discussion
1. What can you tell me about these leaves?
2. What is the same about these leaves?
3. What is different about some of the leaves?
4. What can you say about the color of these leaves?
5. What can you know from touching the leaves?
6. What can you say about the shapes of the leaves?
7. How long was your longest/shortest leaf?
8. Why did different people have different measurements for their leaves?
9. How did the leaf look different when you looked through the magnifying lens?

XI. Extensions

1. Students place leaves in sets according to length, width, color, shape, pattern, etc.
2. Students use leaves to make up their own whole number computations.
3. Students stack up leaves in groups of two, five or ten and measure the height of stacks.
4. Students measure the area of a leaf by tracing around the leaf on graph paper.

XII. Curriculum Coordinates

Language Arts

1. Students will finish the sentence—"If I were a leaf, I would..."
2. Begin a contest to see who can bring in the largest, smallest, strangest, etc. leaf.
3. Use the large leaf pattern to write leaf books.

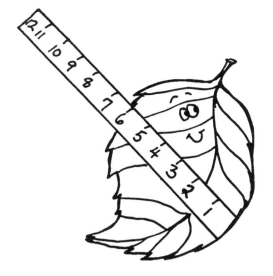

Fall Leafs Me. Happy

Please, measure four (4) leaves:

1 _____ inches

2 _____ inches

3 _____ inches

4 _____ inches

Draw a picture of what your favorite leaf looked like under the magnifying glass:

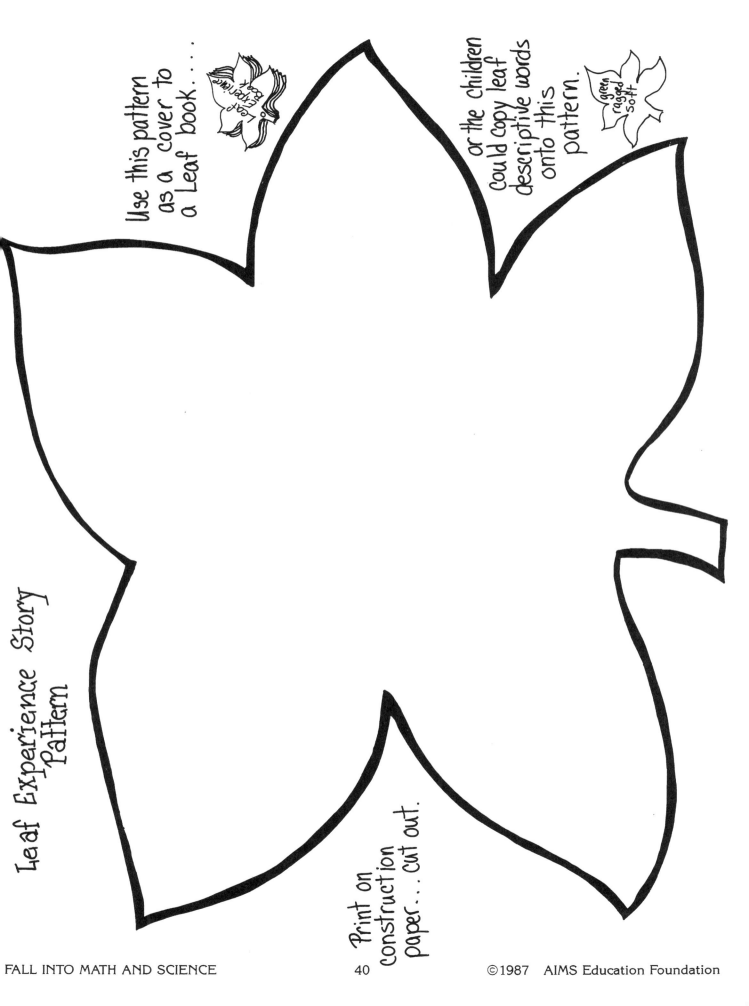

Leaf Experience Story Pattern

Use this pattern as a cover to a Leaf book....

Leaf Experience book

or the children could copy leaf descriptive words onto this pattern.

green ragged soft

Print on construction paper... cut out.

 # Leaf the Dyeing to Us!

I. Topic Area
Holidays: Thanksgiving/Easter
Natural Food Dyes

II. Introductory Statement
Students will learn how color dyes are made from food.

III. Key Question
How can we make dyes to change the colors of these objects?

IV. Math Skills
a. Using a formula
b. Predicting
c. Observing
d. Measuring
e. Graphing
  1. Whole number computation
  2. Solving simple equations
  3. Recording data
  4. Interpreting data
  5. Counting

V. Materials
- Various foods for dyes (see background information)
- Hot plate or other type of heat source
- Pot with lid
- Water
- Small containers to hold dyes
- For Easter eggs: 1-2 egg(s) per child
    vinegar (helps dye adhere to egg)
- For Thanksgiving: bird feathers
    fabric (needs to be 100% cotton)
    macaroni
    manufactured food coloring
- Posterboard for graph
- Construction paper squares with colors corresponding to match the dyes (1 of each color per child)

VI. Background Information
1. The following foods will make natural dyes when boiled in water:
   - Red Cabbage ....blue
   - Blackberries ....blue
   - Cranberries...........................red
   - Beets ....red-violet
   - Onions.......................red or yellow
   - Rhubarb Leaves ....light green
   - Spinach Leaves....................green
2. An approximate proportion of water to food is three parts water to two parts food.
3. The water and food need to be brought to a full boil, then simmered for at least one hour to make a dye strong enough to color the desired objects.
4. The dyes to be made are extremely pale. You may wish to add commercial food coloring to the natural dye in order to make a dye strong enough for all materials.

VII. Management
1. This activity works well if one dye is to be made each day over a one week period, with the actual dyeing process conducted on Friday.
2. The teacher should be in charge of stirring the dyes and placing all food in the boiling water.
3. The children need to be instructed to take great care in handling all dyes—they will stain clothing.

VIII. Advanced Preparation
1. Purchase and clean vegetables and fruit to be used. Measure three parts water per two parts food ingredient.
2. Prepare classroom graph and construction paper markers for graph (one color per child, per dye).

IX. Procedure
1. Distribute construction paper markers to each child.
2. As the teacher names and shows each food item, children predict what color dye that food will make and place the corresponding marker on the graph.
3. Place food item in water on hot plate and bring to boil. Reduce heat and simmer for one hour. When the dye has cooled, remove the food from the pot and discard. Pour the dye into the desired container.
4. Students observe dye and check prediction chart to see the number of correct and incorrect predictions. Language extension sentences using addition, subtraction, and classification could be used at this time.
5. If you desire to make varying colors on other days, merely repeat steps 1-4.
6. Students will used the dyes to color desired objects by placing the objects in containers and leaving them there until the desired color is attained. Commercial food coloring may be added at this time in order to produce a brighter and longer lasting dye.

X. Discussion
1. What made the color change in the water?
2. What would happen if we added more or less water?
3. What other things could we possibly use to make natural dyes?

 Red Cabbage

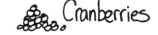 Cranberries

XII. Curriculum Coordinates

Language Arts

1. Make language experience books entitled, "My Favorite Color," or "If I Were an Easter Egg."

Physical Education

1. Play a version of Hide-and-Go-Seek where the children are hidden Easter eggs (or Indians), and the Easter Bunny (or Pilgrims) go hunting for them.

Social Studies

1. Use this activity as part of a unit on Native Americans in November.

Art

1. Have the children trace a large pattern of an Easter egg or turkey on colored construction paper. Decorate and create patterns on the paper with "Goofy Goop" in squeeze bottles.

Goofy Goop

1 cup flour
1 cup salt
1 cup water
desired food coloring

Mix flour, salt, and water. Separate batter and place in squeeze bottles. Add desired food coloring, and mix. Squeeze onto desired pattern. Allow the project to dry 2 to 3 hours or longer before handling.

Leaf the Dyeing to Us!

* Red Cabbage - blue
* Blackberries - blue
* Cranberries - Red
* Beets - red-violet
* Onions - red or yellow
* Rhurbarb leaves - light green
* Spinach leaves - green

Make construction paper markers for each color you are making, for each child. (1" x 1")

Red Cabbage	▨ ☐ ☐ ☐ ▨ ☐ ▨ ☐
Cranberries	☐ ▨ ▨ ▨ ▨ ▨ ▨ ☐
Spinach	▨ ▨ ▨ ▨ ☐ ☐ ☐ ☐
	← If you are doing 1 dye per day, you can add each name and predict daily.
	↓

As the teacher names and shows each food item, children predict what color dye that food will make and place the corresponding marker on the graph.

Make the dye.

Students observe the dye and check the prediction chart to see the number of correct and incorrect predictions. Language extension sentences using addition, subtraction, and classification could be used at this time.

* Making the Dye:

Place food items in water on the hot plate and bring to a boil. Reduce heat and simmer for 1 hour. When done, let dye cool, then remove the food from the pot and discard. Place dye into desired container.

Don't Leaf Out the Vegetables

I. Topic Area
Leaves

II. Introductory Statement
The students will learn that certain types of leaves are edible.

III. Key Question
How many uses can we think of for leaves?

IV. Math Skills
a. Graphing
1. Whole number computation
2. Solving simple equations
3. Using a formula
4. Ordinal numbers
5. Predicting
6. Counting
7. Interpreting data
b. Equations
c. Sorting
d. Observing
e. Sampling

Science Processes
a. Observing and classifying
b. Controlling variables
c. Gathering and recording data
d. Interpreting data
e. Applying and generalizing

V. Materials
• A variety of edible leaves (see background information for suggestions)
• Knife to chop vegetables
• Butcher paper for graph
• One graph marker per child (leaf patterns provided)
• One brad and extra leaf pattern for each vegetable to be tasted

VI. Background Information
The following foods are considered to be leafy vegetables and are edible:

Lettuce: romaine, butter, iceberg, red
Cabbage: regular, chinese, red
Brussel Srpouts
Parsley
Mustard Greens
Collard Greens
Swiss Chard
Spinach
Tofu
Endive

VII. Management
1. This activity works well in a whole class situation with direct teacher supervision.
2. The discussion, tasting, and graphing activities will take approximately 45 minutes-1 hour.

VIII. Advanced Preparation
1. Purchase, clean, and chop desired vegetables.
2. Prepare classroom graph and markers.

IX. Procedure
1. The teacher asks the key question, "What kinds of uses can you think of for leaves?" The teacher lists the responses on the chalkboard or chart paper. If eating is not mentioned, the teacher should suggest this possibility. It is extremely important to emphasize to the children that not all leaves are edible, and that no leaf should ever be placed in the mouth unless approved by a responsible adult.
2. The teacher displays one leaf at a time. Each leaf is described on the basis of size, color, texture, smell and finally taste. Do not tell the children what kind of leafy vegetable each is until the graph is completed and discussed. Continue in this manner until each leaf has been discussed and tasted.
3. After all the leaves have been tasted, review the look of each leaf with the entire class and allow the children to select their favorite tasting leaf.
4. Have each child place his/her marker in the column above their leaf preference.
5. Discuss the results.
6. Expose the name of each leaf and discuss.

X. Discussion
1. Are all leaves edible? What kind of leaves can be eaten? What kinds cannot?
2. What other kinds of leafy vegetables could be eaten?
3. Are people the only things that can eat leaves?

XI. Extensions
Graphing ideas: Allow each child to taste each kind of leaf and tell him/her its name. Blindfold the taster and have him/her identify each leaf by taste.

XII. **Curriculum Coordinates**

Language Arts

1. Read the story "The Giving Tree" by Shel Silverstein.
2. Visit a supermarket and observe its produce department. Write language experience stories about the trip.

Science

1. Go on a nature walk and collect and classify leaves.
2. Plant and maintain a vegetable garden.

Physical Education

1. Play a version of the game "Freeze". Have the children pretend they are leaves falling from a tree. When a bell is rung, they must freeze in whatever position they happen to be in at that moment.

Music

Sing "Crunchy Leaves" or "Whirly Twirly"

Art

1. Make leaf rubbings by holding various shaped leaves under paper and rubbing crayons over the top.
2. Make leaf silhouettes. Place a leaf on a piece of white construction paper. Rub a piece of sponge that has been dipped in autumn colors of paint over the edges of the leaf, continuing onto the paper. Continue in this manner until the entire outline of the leaf has been transferred to the paper.

Don't Leaf Out the Vegetables
Class Graph

Construction Paper Markers

Butcher Paper

Cover the name of each vegetable with a leaf pattern and a brad until the end of the discussion period.

Look	Taste	Look	Taste	Look	Taste
green wrinkled ragged	sweet crunchy	floppy large	sour crisp	dark green small pointed	good wet moist

Leaves: Ron, Heidi, Grant, Brett, Eric, 1 / Lisa, Sherry, 2 / Carrie, Jenny, Brian, 3

The teacher displays one leaf at a time. Each leaf is described by its size, color, texture, smell, and finally taste. Record the children's language on the graph. Use later for a story or just review. After all the leaves have been tasted, allow the children to select their favorite tasting leaf. Have each child place a leaf marker above their preference. Discuss results. Reveal the name of each leaf and discuss.

Make sure when you chop the vegetables, you leave 1 leaf whole to display!

Spinning Ghosts

I. Topic Area
Air

II. Introductory Statement
Students will learn how to make a paper ghost spin.

III. Key Question
What can we do to this paper ghost to make it spin?

IV. Math Skills / Science Processes

Math Skills
a. Predicting
b. Graphing
  1. Counting
  2. Whole number computation
  3. Interpreting data

Science Processes
a. Observing and classifying
b. Controlling data
c. Gathering and recording data
d. Interpreting data
e. Applying and generalizing

V. Materials
- 5 paper ghosts cut from construction paper or bond paper
- Prediction graph
- Paper clips (metal)
- Markers for graph (one for each student)

VI. Background Information
Paper thickness has an effect on the way the ghosts spin. Ghosts made from lighter paper usually spin better than those made from heavier paper.

Before beginning this investigation with your class, you may want to tell them a story about a little ghost who wanted to "spin" instead of "float".

VII. Management
1. This activity takes about 15-20 minutes.
2. It is a whole group activity.

VIII. Advanced Preparation
1. Prepare the prediction graph. See page 51.
2. Cut out 5 ghosts. (Use ghost pattern #1.)
  a. Attach a paper clip to the bottom of the first ghost and glue the ghost to the top of section 1 on the graph.
  b. Attach a paper clip to the bottom of the second ghost and fold both of its arms forward. Glue this ghost to the top of section 2 on the graph.
  c. Attach a paper clip to the bottom of the third ghost and fold one of its arms forward and the other backwards. Glue this ghost to the top of section 3.
  d. Glue the fourth ghost to the top of section 4. Do not fold it or add a paper clip.
  e. The fifth ghost is to be used for the demonstration.
3. Make one $1'' \times 2\frac{1}{2}''$ paper marker for each student. Put names on them.

IX. Procedure
1. Hold up the paper ghost and explain to the students that the ghost you are holding can only "float" to the ground. Demonstrate this by letting go of the ghost. Have the students comment on what they observe.
2. Tell the class that you want to make the ghost spin around as it floats down. Have the students think of ways to make the ghost spin. (You may want to record these ideas.) It is important to accept all suggestions without indicating whether or not these ideas might work.
3. Show the prediction graph. Explain that the ghost in each section has been changed in the following ways: (1) by adding just a paper clip to the bottom; (2) by adding a paper clip and bending the arms forward; (3) by adding a paper clip and bending one arm forward and the other backwards, and (4) by keeping the ghost just the way it is but by blowing on it as it falls. Have the students show their predictions by placing their markers in the sections they choose.
4. Discuss the graph.
5. Demonstrate each of the ways shown on the graph by adding the paper clip and/or folding the arms and then tossing the ghost in the air. Have the students discuss their observations.

X. Discussion
1. Which was the best way to make the ghost spin? Is that the way most people predicted would be the best?
2. What effect does the paper clip have on making the ghost spin?
3. What are some other things we might try to make the ghost spin?
4. Can you think of other objects that spin? (Windmills, the blades on a helicopter, etc.)

XI. Extensions
1. Give each student a ghost. (Use ghost pattern #2.) See if the children can remember how to fold the arms to make it spin.
2. Have the students experiment with other ways to make the ghost spin.
3. Try using ghosts made from different types of paper. Do they all spin? Which spins the best? Which falls fastest?

XII. Curriculum Coordinates

Language Arts

1. Have the students make up stories about their ghosts.
2. Read books about ghosts. (Robert Bright's books about Georgie, for example)
3. Use the large ghost pattern for students to write their own ghost stories.
4. Teach the fingerplay "Five Little Ghosts."

    Five little ghosts dressed all in white
    Were scaring each other on Halloween night.

    "Boo!" said the first one, "I'll catch you!"
    "Woooo," said the second, "I don't care if you do!"

    The third ghost said, "You can't run away from me."
    The fourth one said, "I'll scare everyone I see."

    The fifth one said, "It's time to disappear.
    See you at Halloween time next year!"

    --Unknown

Art

1. Have the children decorate their ghosts.
2. Use white chalk to make ghosts on black paper.

Physical Education

1. Have the students try spinning around with their arms held at their sides; with their arms out in front of them, and then with their arms straight out from their sides. Discuss which way the students liked best and why.

Spinning Ghosts

A. Prepare the prediction graph:

B. Cut out 5 ghosts (ghost pattern #1)
   1. 1ˢᵗ Ghost — paper clip at bottom
   2. 2ⁿᵈ Ghost — paper clip at bottom, fold both arms forward
   3. 3ʳᵈ Ghost — paper clip at bottom, one arm forward, one backwards
   4. 4ᵗʰ Ghost — no paper clip, no folds
   5. 5ᵗʰ Ghost — use this ghost for demonstration
      Glue the first 4 ghosts to the prediction graph.

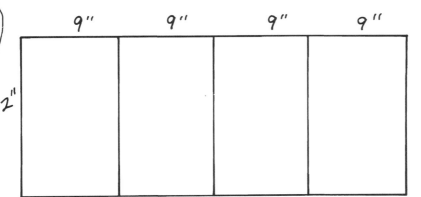

Glue 1 ghost to the top of each section.

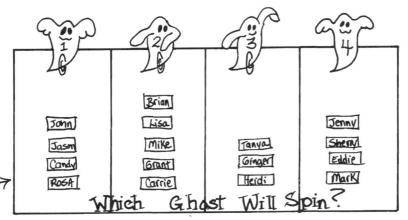

Make a 1" x 2½" paper marker for each student. Put their names on them.

Ask students which ghost they think will spin. Have them show their predictions by placing their markers in the section they choose.

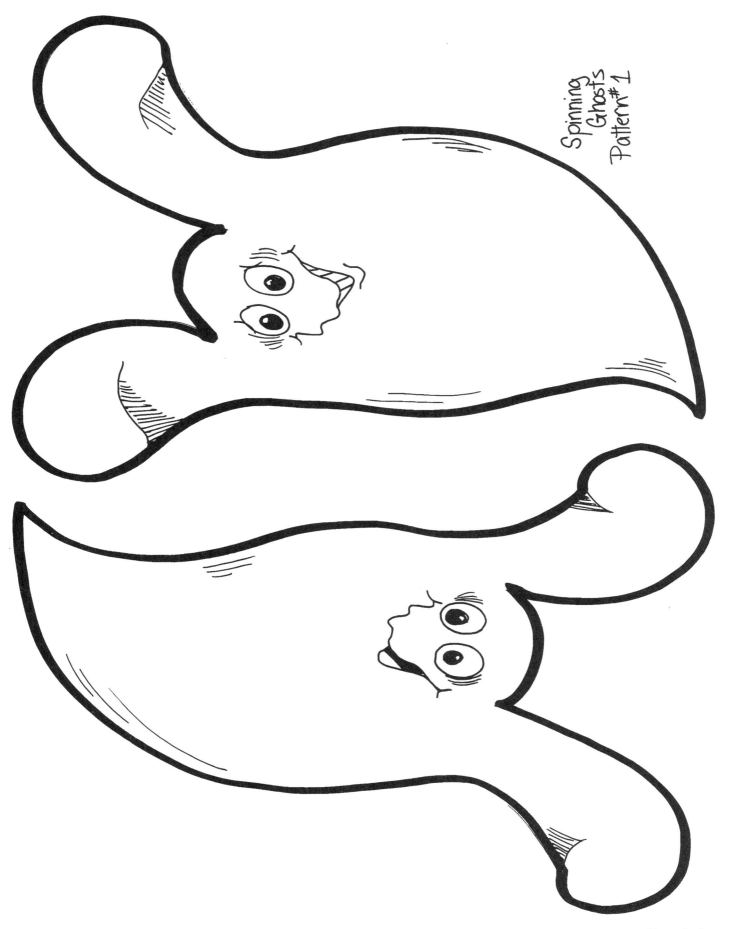

Spinning Ghosts Pattern # 1

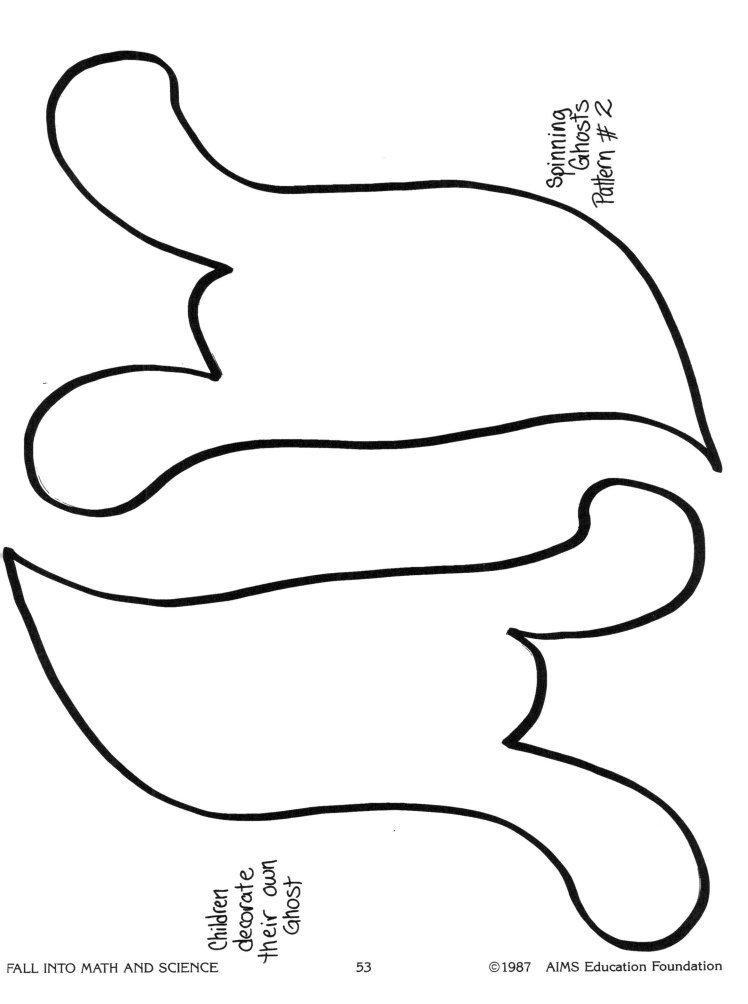

Spinning Ghosts
Pattern # 2

Children
decorate
their own
Ghost

Ghost Pattern #3

Use for cover of children's Ghost Stories

Nicole's Ghost Story

Goody Goody Gumballs

I. Topic Area
Sorting and Classifying

II. Introductory Statement
Students will sort and classify "gumballs" and "jaw-breakers" on a gumball machine.

III. Key Question
How can these gumballs be sorted?

IV. Math Skills
a. Sorting
b. Observing
c. Logical thinking
d. Patterns
e. Estimating

Science Processes
a. Classifying
b. Estimating
c. Interpreting data
d. Comparing

V. Materials
• Gumball machines
• Gumballs and jawbreakers made of paper
• Jars
• Gumballs
• Jawbreakers
• Pattern strips with patterns made with attribute stickers

VII. Management
1. Allow 15 to 20 minutes.
2. This is a small group teacher-directed activity.

VIII. Advanced Preparation
1. Prepare the gumball machines. Mount the gameboards on white construction or tag. Cut out the "glass." Laminate and, by jove, you have a "real" looking gumball machine.
2. Prepare the gumballs and jawbreakers. Make a copy on several assorted colors. Laminate or contact and cut out.
3. Make pattern strips on white construction or tag about 2" by 9". Using attribute stickers, make a different pattern on each strip alternating colors and sizes. Put the missing pattern pieces on 2" × 2" square for the students to complete the patterns.

black   red   black   red   ____ ____

yellow blue red yellow blue   ____ ____

IX. Procedure
1. Before using the gameboards, the previous day or two, fill a baby food jar with real gumballs. The students estimate the number of gumballs.
2. Do the same thing with jawbreakers and let the students estimate.
3. Compare the totals of gumballs and jawbreakers.
4. When using the gumball machines each child will have one in a small group.
5. Put all the assorted colors and two sizes of gumballs and jawbreakers into a pile in the middle.
6. Invite the students to think about whay they see. How are some the same? How are some different? What about colors? Sizes?
7. Give each child a handful of gumballs and jawbreakers and have them sort them into sets in their gumball machine. The students will need to be able to state why they sorted as they did.

X. Discussion
1. Can the gumballs and jawbreakers be sorted in different ways? Why?
2. Is there more than one right way?
3. What if we had buttons to sort? Could we sort in some more ways? Keys? Bottle caps? etc.

XI. Extension
1. Use the gumball machines with a set of task cards. Each child has a gameboard in front of him/her. The teacher uses task cards to practice whatever skill the group needs, for example: number recognition, combinations, number words, reading words, etc. For each correct response the child places a gumball in his/her machine. The child with the most gumballs is the winner.

57

Print these on yellow, red, blue, green, construction paper.

Cut out.

Jawbreakers

gumballs

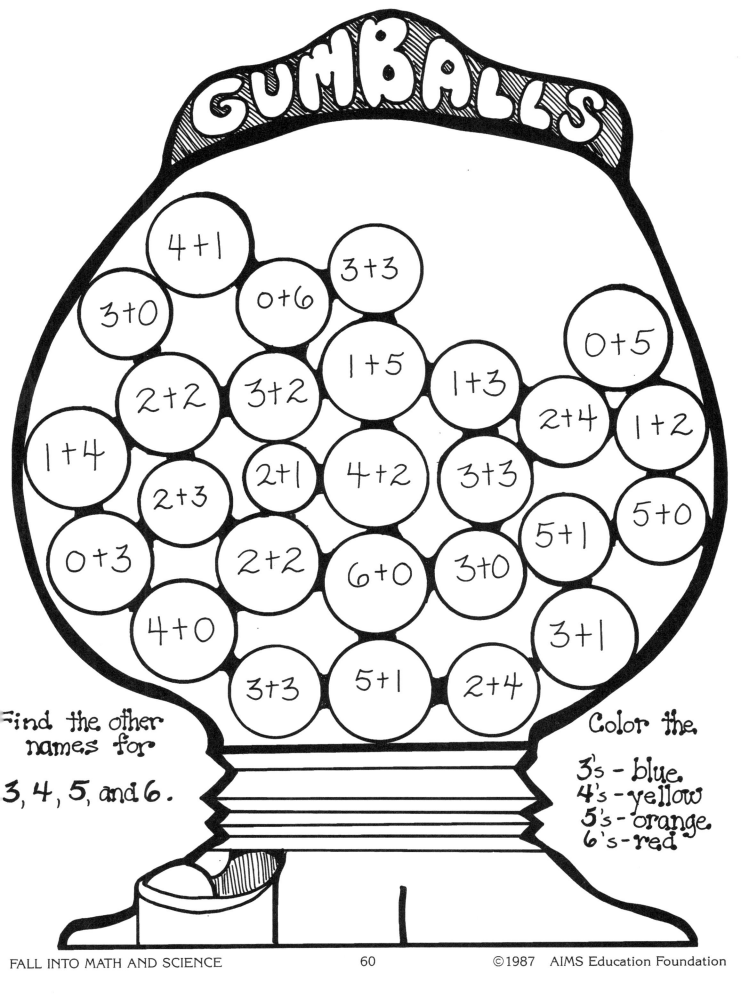

GUMBALLS

4+1
3+0
0+6
3+3
0+5
2+2
3+2
1+5
1+3
2+4
1+2
1+4
2+3
2+1
4+2
3+3
5+0
0+3
2+2
6+0
3+0
5+1
4+0
3+1
3+3
5+1
2+4

Find the other names for 3, 4, 5, and 6.

Color the
3's - blue
4's - yellow
5's - orange
6's - red

You Drive Me Crackers

I. Topic Area
Sorting and Classifying

II. Introductory Statement
Students will sort and classify by shapes four kinds of crackers.

III. Key Question
How could we group these crackers?

IV. Math Skills

Math Skills
a. Estimating
b. Predicting
c. Sorting and classifying
d. Geometry
e. Graphing
  1. Counting
  2. Recording data

Science Processes
a. Observing
b. Estimating
c. Interpreting data
d. Applying and generalizing

V. Materials
- Four boxes of crackers: Bacon Thins (oval); Wheat Wafers (square); Ritz (circle); and Waverly Wafers (rectangle)
- Sorting sheet (see attached)
- Graph paper (see attached)
- Baggies (one for each child)
- Crayons
- Two charts (18 × 24), one for predictions and one for actual count
- Gummed circles, two colors

VII. Management
1. Allow 15 to 20 minutes.
2. This is a small group teacher-directed activity.

VIII. Advanced Preparation
1. Prepare sorting papers.
2. Prepare graphs.
3. Place an assortment of shape crackers in a baggie for each child.
4. Separate two sheets of paper approximately 18 × 24 into eight columns.

IX. Procedure
1. Show one shape at a time and have the students make a prediction of which shape will have the most by placing a gummed circle in the proper column.
2. Students are given a baggie with an assortment of the four shapes.
3. Students sort the shape crackers on the sorting sheet.
4. Place the crackers on the individual graph paper according to the classification.
5. Students remove each cracker and color in the corresponding square to form a representation of a real graph.
6. Place circles in the column that tells of which shape there was the most on each individual graph.

X. Discussion
1. What does the prediction chart show?
2. What does the actual chart show?
3. How can we make these shapes disappear?

XI. Extension
1. Use another assortment of shape crackers and have the students estimate the number of crackers.
2. Use attached paper of shapes and make copies for the children in four colors: red, yellow, blue, and green. Teacher can ask the children to show him/her the shapes that are red, shapes that are triangles, shapes that are green, etc. Make the directions more complex, such as show me all the large, yellow shapes; large, blue shapes with four sides, etc.

XII. Curriculum Coordinates
Language Arts
1. Make a class book of shapes. Example: Triangle Book. △ Each page is the shape of a triangle and the students draw something that is a triangle and dictates their story to the teacher. The pages are assembled into one book. Do this for each shape.

Music
1. Use a simple tune all the children know, or make up a tune with the children. Example: Old Mac-Donald Had a Farm.

  We are marching on the square,
    Marching on the square.
  We are marching on the square,
    Marching on the square.
  We are marching on the triangle,
    Marching on the triangle...etc.
  We are marching 'round the circle,
    'Round and 'round and 'round...etc.
  We are marching on the rectangle,
    On the rectangle...etc.

Tune: Mary Had a Little Lamb

We are marching 'round the circle,
　'Round the circle, 'round the circle,
We are marching 'round the circle,
　'Round and 'round and 'round.
(Use the other shapes.)

Physical Education

1. Draw a line, use masking tape, or a rope to make large shapes on the floor or blacktop, etc. Make the shapes as large as space allows. When using a rope, start with a line and gradually close the ends so the children can feel the closure with their bodies as they move around the shape. Chant the name of the shape as they move around the shape.

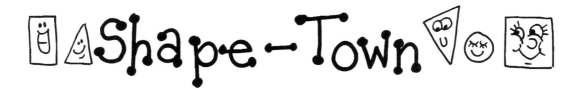

Flannel Board Story for shapes. You will need to make assorted sizes and colors of shapes.

Here are the squares □ □ □ □ □.
They live all by themselves in Square Town.

Here are the circles ○ ○ ○ ○ ○.
They live all by themselves in Circle Town.

Here are the triangles △ △ △ △ △.
They live all by themselves in Triangle Town.

Here are the rectangles ▭ ▭ ▭ ▭.
They live all by themselves in Rectangle Town.

The squares do not like the circles.

The circles do not like the triangles.

The rectangles do not like the squares.

They do not like anyone but themselves. They think the others are lazy and mean and bad! bad! bad!

The squares say this, "If you want to be smart, beautiful and good you must have four sides exactly the same. If you don't have four sides exactly the same, then you are lazy and ugly and bad! bad! bad!

The circles say this, "If you want to be smart, beautiful and good you must be perfectly round. If you aren't perfectly round, then you are lazy and ugly and bad! bad! bad!

The triangles say this, "If you want to be smart, beautiful and good you must have only three side. If you don't have three sides then you are lazy and ugly and bad! bad! bad!

The rectangles say this, "If you want to be smart, beautiful and good you must have 2 sides short exactly the same and 2 sides long exactly the same. If you don't have 2 sides short exactly the same and 2 sides long exactly the same, then you are ugly and lazy and bad! bad! bad!

One beautiful summer day the little squares and circles, the triangles and the rectangles went outside to play. But NOT together!

While they were playing a terrible thing happened! The circles were playing on top of the hill. Some of them slipped and went rolling down the hill. They rolled down the hill to where the rectangles were playing.

The rectangles were very angry. They thought the circles were rude, so they called the circles names and threw rocks at them. The circles were frightened. The squares and the triangles heard the yelling and crying. They ran to the bottom of the hill. At last one of the rectangles became so angry that he leaped into the air and came down right on top of the circles! Guess what happened? Everything was quiet! No one said a word! They just looked and looked and looked. The rectangle and two circles made a wagon.

Everyone was excited. They all wanted to do something. The circles and squares made a train. The rectangles made a smoke stack. Some tiny o's made smoke.

The triangles and rectangles made trees.

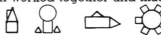

They all worked together and made these things:

When it was time to go home they all sang a little song: "We are glad, glad, glad. Being different isn't bad, bad, bad." And they sang it over and over all the way home!

You Drive Me Crackers

1. Prepare the class graph:
2. Divide the graph into 4 major groups: (4 sheets of construction or tag) circle, square, oval, rectangle.
3. You may want to glue the cracker to its shape on the graph.
4. Divide each major column into two columns — one for predictions of most common shape and one for actual count.
5. Use gummed circles for graph — 1 color for predictions, 1 for actual count.

	12"		12"		12"		12"
We think:	We counted:	We think:	We counted:	We think:	We counted:	We think:	We counted:
					◍		
		○			◍		
		○			◍	○	
	◍	○			◍	○	◍
	◍	○		○	◍	○	◍
○	◍	○	◍	○	◍	○	◍
○	◍	○	◍	○	◍	○	◍
○	◍	○	◍	○	◍	○	◍
○	◍	○	◍	○	◍	○	◍
circle		square		oval		rectangle	

Show one shape at a time and have students make a prediction of which shape will have the most by placing a gummed circle over that shape. Hand out baggies of crackers.

After sorting and making their own graphs, students will place a different colored gummed circle over the shape that was the most common in their own sample.

Sorting Sheet

square

circle

oval

rectangle

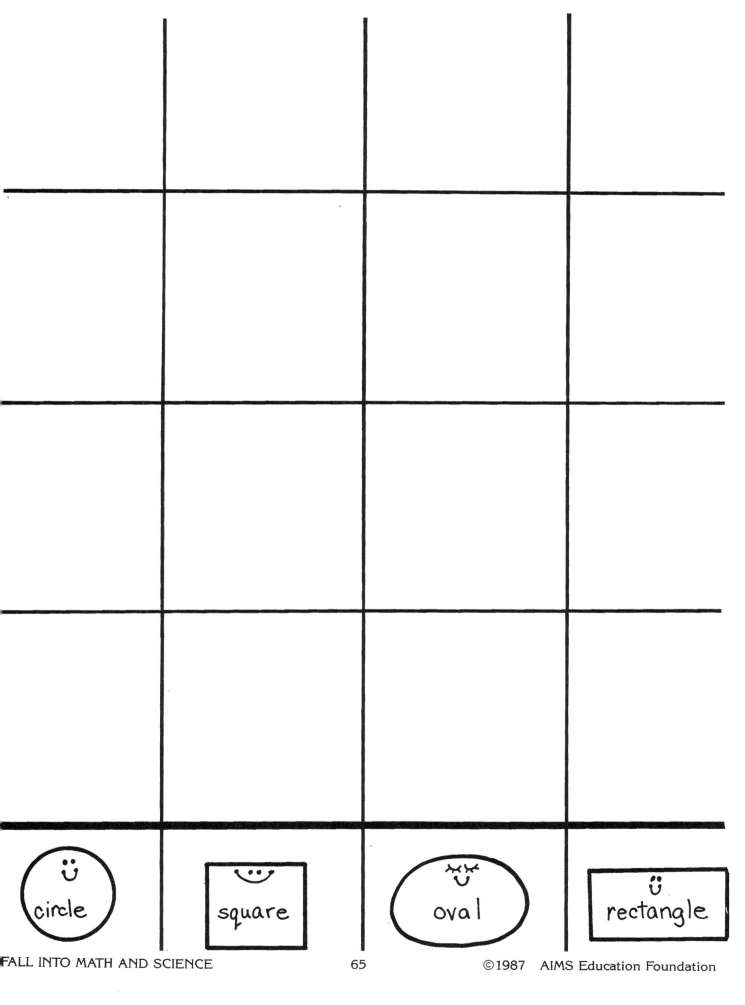

circle

square

oval

rectangle

Shape Land

I can count :

___ O's   ___ △'s

___ □'s   ___ ▭'s

name: _____

Shape Up!

I. Topic Area
Shapes

II. Introductory Statement
Students will predict where shapes belong.

III. Key Question
Where do you think the shapes will go?

IV. Math Skills
a. Predicting
b. Logical thinking
c. Observing
d. Problem solving
e. Generalizing
f. Attributes

Science Processes
a. Gathering and recording data
b. Interpreting data
c. Observing and classifying
d. Comparing

V. Materials
- Geometric shapes (see worksheets) or use materials such as Relationshapes (plastic shapes of assorted sizes, colors, and thicknesses)
- One red and blue unifix cube for each child
- One piece of 9 × 12 red construction paper
- One piece of blue 9 × 12 construction paper

VII. Management
1. Allow 15 to 20 minutes for the group
2. This is a small-group teacher directed activity.

VIII. Advanced Preparation
1. Prepare shapes from the worksheets so you will have different sizes and colors of the shapes. (Thicknesses of shapes are optional.)

IX. Procedure
1. Place some shapes on the red paper and some other shapes on the blue paper according to the same attibute.

Example:

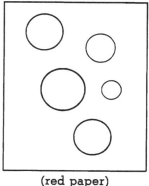

(red paper)

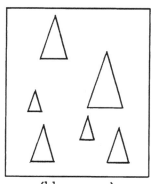

(blue paper)

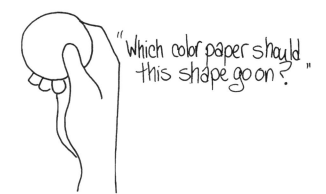

"Which color paper should this shape go on?"

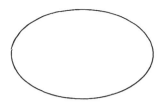
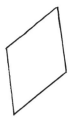

2. Hold up a shape you are going to place on one of the papers. Look at the children as you do this and pretend you are going to place the shape on both papers.

3. The children try to guess what you are thinking and predict where you will put the shape.

4. The children predict with their unifix cubes and hold up the red cube if they think the shape will go on the red paper or hold up the blue cube if they think the shape belongs on the blue paper.

5. Continue this way until all the shapes are placed.

6. Each of the children will be involved with his/her unifix cubes, thinking for himself/herself. The teacher can observe which of the children can discover the attributes.

7. Repeat many times using many different attributes.

X. Discussion

1. Did it matter about the *color* when I was thinking about the shapes? *size*? *thickness*?

2. How are they the same? different?

3. Why are there some shapes on the red paper that are not on the blue paper?

XI. Extensions

1. Let the children explore with wooden or plastic parquetry blocks or attribute blocks. Match pattern cards.

2. Cut up shapes to match the attibute blocks and let the children make a pattern with paper shapes to match a pattern made with attribute blocks.

3. Frog and Shapes Game
Scatter shapes on the floor or a table top. Using a paper frog ask one child at a time to have the frog "hop" to a large red triangle, a small green circle, etc.

XII. Curriculum Coordinates

Language Arts

For language development make a large triangle (or rectangle, square, circle, etc.) on the floor. Start the activity by assigning children to various shapes with math vocabulary building terms...

"All those wearing blue may stand with toes (or heels) on the line of the _____"(name shape)

"All those with brown shoes may stand with toes (or heels) on the line of the _____"(name shape)

"If you are _____ years old stand in the center of the _____"

"If your name begins with _____, stand _____.": etc.

"If you have one sister (or two brothers, one sister and two brothers, or any combination, etc.) stand on the _____."

"These three people may hold up three fingers and stand with toes (heels) on the line of the triangle."

"How many children do we need for one to stand on each angle of the rectangle? triangle? square?"

To paraphrase Confucius: "He who has made square with the seat of pants KNOWS what squareness is."

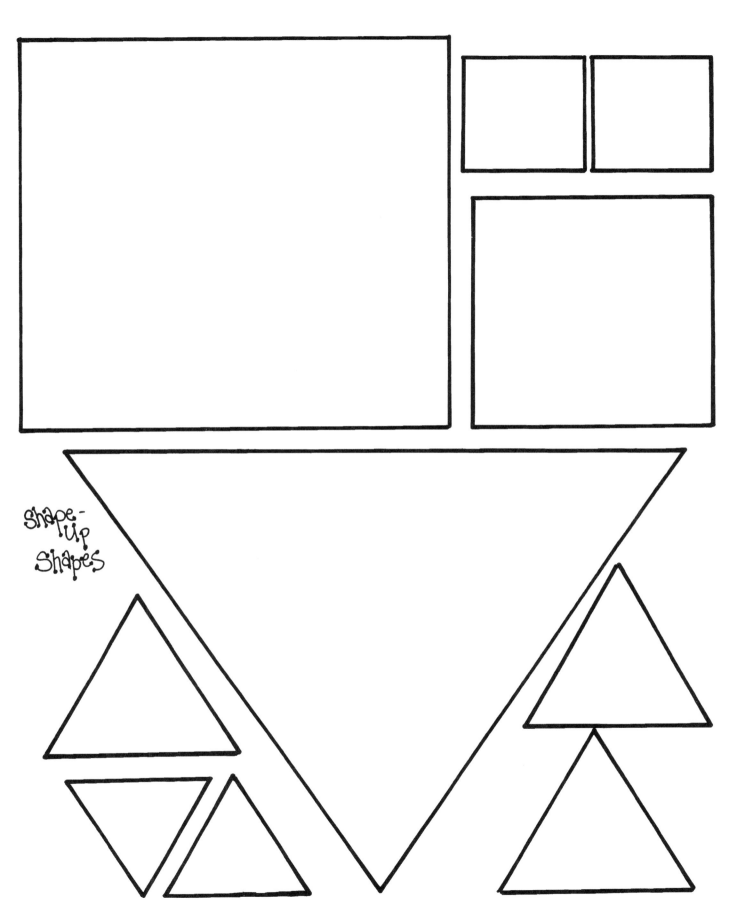

Shape-up Shapes

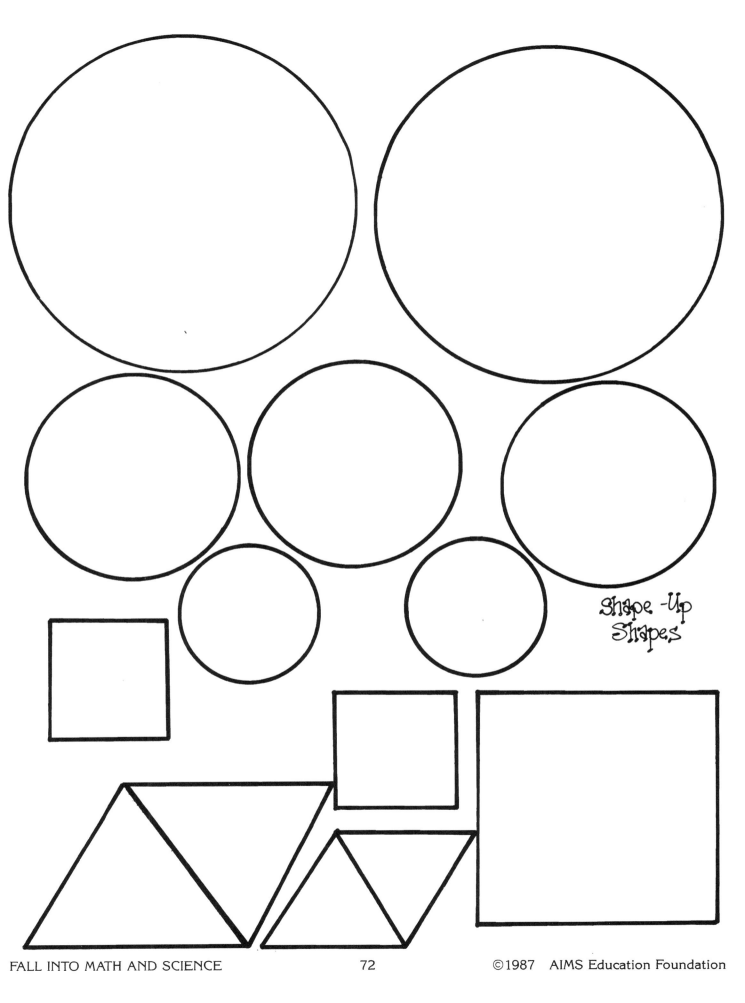

Shape-Up
Shapes

Going Nuts

I. Topic Area
Food

II. Introductory Statement
Students will learn about the attributes and tastes of different nuts.

III. Key Question
What can we find out about these nuts?

IV. Math Skills

a. Attributes
b. Generalizing
c. Graphing
   1. Counting
   2. Interpreting data
   3. Logical thinking
d. Observing
e. Patterns
f. Sorting

Science Processes

a. Observing and classifying
b. Gathering and recording data
c. Interpreting data
d. Applying and generalizing
e. Comparing

V. Materials
- various shelled nuts—brought by students
- floor graph
- pattern cards
- nut shapes (see pattern pages)
- nutcracker

VI. Background Information
1. Peanuts grow underground and therefore are not true nuts.

VII. Management
1. Teacher will need to send a note home several days in advance asking students to bring various nuts to school.
2. This investigation is a three day project, taking 20-30 minutes per day.

VIII. Advanced Preparation
1. Prepare and send home a note asking students to bring assorted nuts to school. (See example at end of investigation.)
2. Prepare a floor graph with space for placing various nuts. (See example.)

Walnuts	Almonds	Peanuts	Pistachios

✳

3. Prepare pattern cards and nut patterns.

IX. Procedure
1. On first day of investigation, gather children around graph, sort nuts and place on floor graph. Lead children in discussion about graph. See X. *Discussion.*
2. Help children change the real graph to a representational graph by drawing pictures of nuts corresponding to the number of nuts. Place the representational graph on chalkboard.
3. On second day of investigation, show students an example of a pattern card and ask them to make their own patterns. See example.

✳
✳

- Teacher may want to make up pattern cards for each student, (with two examples of the pattern), if students are not familiar with pattern cards.

4. On the third day of the investigation, students meet in small groups and talk about the attributes of the nuts. Students may also taste each type of nut. Allow students to discuss freely their observations about the attributes and tastes of each nut. See X. *Discussion.*
5. Use a nutcracker to crack the harder nuts, and allow the students to crack the easier nuts, such as peanuts and pistachios.

X. Discussion
1. What can we find out about these nuts?
2. How can we sort out these nuts?
3. How many walnuts...peanuts...almonds...etc. do we have?
4. Which nut is there more of? Which nut is there less of?
5. How can we show how many nuts we have if we want to remove the nuts and put the graph up on the board.
6. What kind of pattern can you make using the shapes of nuts?
7. What can we say about these nuts that are the same...different?
8. Which nut do you like best? Why?
9. Where do you think these nuts come from?

XI. **Extensions**

1. Students may make a graph of their favorite nut.
2. Students may make a list of foods that have nuts in them.

XII. **Curriculum Coordinates**

Social Studies

1. This investigation may be coordinated with a unit on Indians during Thanksgiving time. Students will learn that Indians found their food in their own environment and ate many foods without cooking them.

Going Nuts

Walnuts	Almonds	Peanuts	Pistachios	Hazelnuts
🥜	🌰	🥜	🌰	🌰
🥜	🌰	🥜	🌰	🌰
🥜	🌰	🥜	🌰	🌰
🥜	🌰	🥜	🌰	🌰
🥜	🌰		🌰	🌰
🥜			🌰	

Floor Graph ⟶ **Wall Graph**

Walnuts	Almonds	Peanuts	Pistachios	Hazelnuts
🥜	🌰	🥜	🌰	🌰
🥜	🌰	🥜	🌰	🌰
🥜	🌰	🥜	🌰	🌰
🥜	🌰	🥜	🌰	🌰
🥜	🌰		🌰	🌰
🥜			🌰	

* On the first day of the investigation, gather the children around the graph, sort the nuts and place on the floor graph. Lead students in a discussion about the graph.

Help the children change the real graph to a representational graph by drawing pictures of nuts corresponding to the number of nuts. Place the representational graph on the chalkboard.

* On the second day, print the nut pattern page. Show students examples of pattern cards, ask them to make their own patterns.

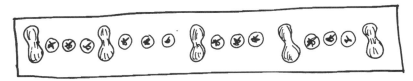

* On the third day, students meet in small groups and discuss attributes of nuts. Students also may taste each type of nut.

Dear Parents,

On Monday, we will be doing a special math-science investigation. This investigation is called "GOING NUTS". We will be using nuts to sort, graph, discuss attributes, and taste. In order to provide for the investigation, we need each child to bring 4 or 5 nuts of one kind. The nuts may be walnuts, almonds, peanuts, hazelnuts, pistachios, or pecans. Please do not send more than 4 or 5 nuts with your child. If each child participates, we will have more than enough.

Please send the nuts by Friday. Thank you for your cooperation. If you have any questions, please call me at school.

Thank you,

Your child's teacher

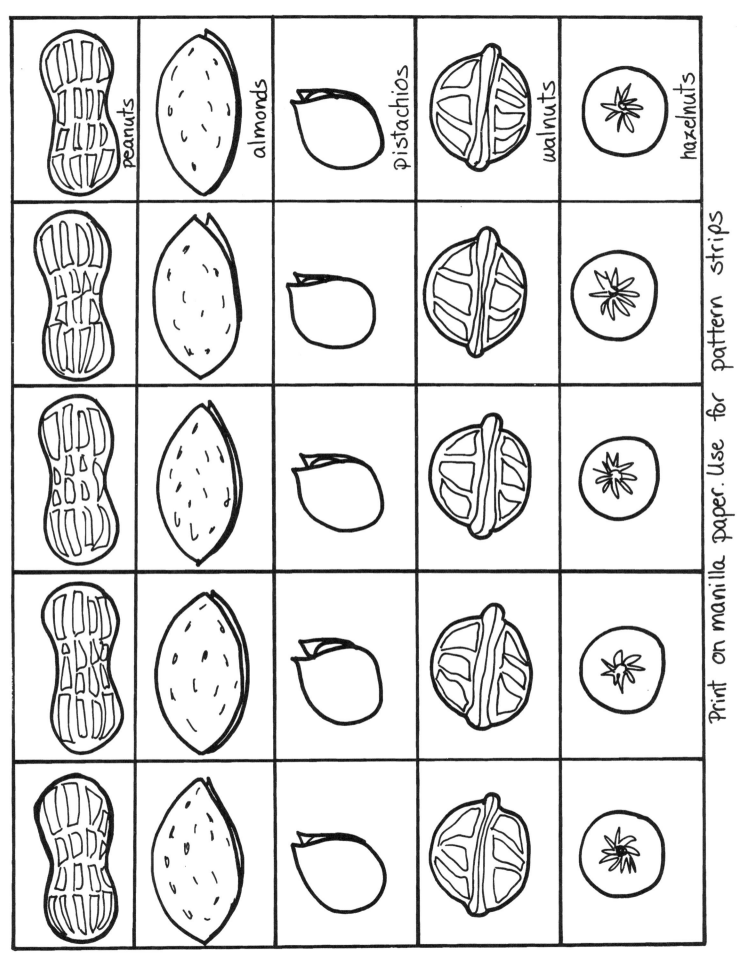

Print on manilla paper. Use for pattern strips

Draw a Nutty Face!

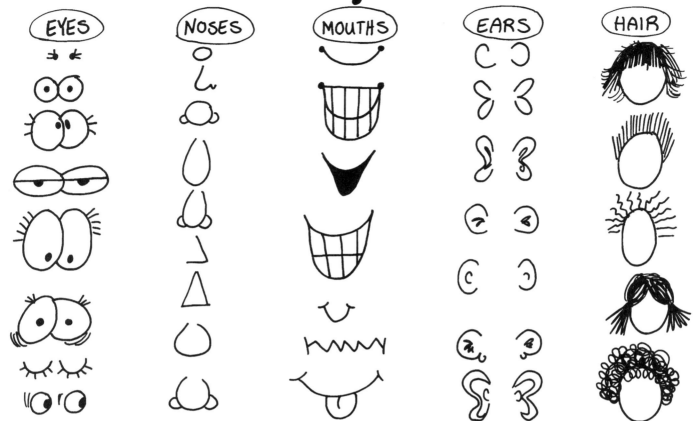

EYES NOSES MOUTHS EARS HAIR

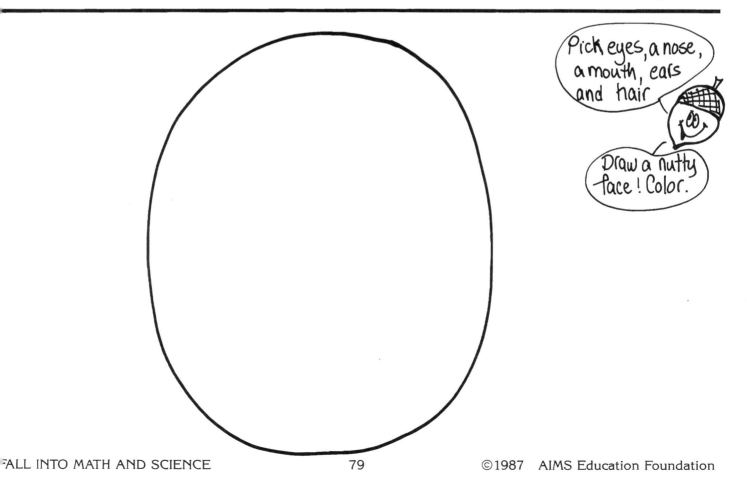

Pick eyes, a nose, a mouth, ears and hair

Draw a nutty face! Color.

The AIMS Program

AIMS is the acronym for "Activities Integrating Mathematics and Science." Such integration enriches learning and makes it meaningful and holistic. AIMS began as a project of Fresno Pacific University to integrate the study of mathematics and science in grades K-9, but has since expanded to include language arts, social studies, and other disciplines.

AIMS is a continuing program of the non-profit AIMS Education Foundation. It had its inception in a National Science Foundation funded program whose purpose was to explore the effectiveness of integrating mathematics and science. The project directors in cooperation with 80 elementary classroom teachers devoted two years to a thorough field-testing of the results and implications of integration.

The approach met with such positive results that the decision was made to launch a program to create instructional materials incorporating this concept. Despite the fact that thoughtful educators have long recommended an integrative approach, very little appropriate material was available in 1981 when the project began. A series of writing projects have ensued, and today the AIMS Education Foundation is committed to continue the creation of new integrated activities on a permanent basis.

The AIMS program is funded through the sale of books, products, and staff development workshops and through proceeds from the Foundation's endowment. All net income from program and products flows into a trust fund administered by the AIMS Education Foundation. Use of these funds is restricted to support of research, development, and publication of new materials. Writers donate all their rights to the Foundation to support its on-going program. No royalties are paid to the writers.

The rationale for integration lies in the fact that science, mathematics, language arts, social studies, etc., are integrally interwoven in the real world from which it follows that they should be similarly treated in the classroom where we are preparing students to live in that world. Teachers who use the AIMS program give enthusiastic endorsement to the effectiveness of this approach.

Science encompasses the art of questioning, investigating, hypothesizing, discovering, and communicating. Mathematics is the language that provides clarity, objectivity, and understanding. The language arts provide us powerful tools of communication. Many of the major contemporary societal issues stem from advancements in science and must be studied in the context of the social sciences. Therefore, it is timely that all of us take seriously a more holistic mode of educating our students. This goal motivates all who are associated with the AIMS Program. We invite you to join us in this effort.

Meaningful integration of knowledge is a major recommendation coming from the nation's professional science and mathematics associations. The American Association for the Advancement of Science in *Science for All Americans* strongly recommends the integration of mathematics, science, and technology. The National Council of Teachers of Mathematics places strong emphasis on applications of mathematics such as are found in science investigations. AIMS is fully aligned with these recommendations.

Extensive field testing of AIMS investigations confirms these beneficial results:

1. Mathematics becomes more meaningful, hence more useful, when it is applied to situations that interest students.
2. The extent to which science is studied and understood is increased, with a significant economy of time, when mathematics and science are integrated.
3. There is improved quality of learning and retention, supporting the thesis that learning that is meaningful and relevant is more effective.
4. Motivation and involvement are increased dramatically as students investigate real-world situations and participate actively in the process.

We invite you to become part of this classroom teacher movement by using an integrated approach to learning and sharing any suggestions you may have.

The AIMS Program welcomes you!

AIMS Education Foundation Programs

Practical proven strategies to improve student achievement

When you host an AIMS workshop for elementary and middle school educators, you will know your teachers are receiving effective usable training they can apply in their classrooms immediately.

Designed for teachers—AIMS Workshops:

- Correlate to your state standards;
- Address key topic areas, including math content, science content, problem solving, and process skills;
- Teach you how to use AIMS' effective hands-on approach;
- Provide practice of activity-based teaching;
- Address classroom management issues, higher-order thinking skills, and materials;
- Give you AIMS resources; and
- Offer college (graduate-level) credits for many courses.

Aligned to district and administrator needs—AIMS workshops offer:

- Flexible scheduling and grade span options;
- Custom (one-, two-, or three-day) workshops to meet specific schedule, topic and grade-span needs;
- Pre-packaged one-day workshops on most major topics—only $3900 for up to 30 participants (includes all materials and expenses);
- Prepackaged four- or five-day workshops for in-depth math and science training—only $12,300 for up to 30 participants (includes all materials and expenses);
- Sustained staff development, by scheduling workshops throughout the school year and including follow-up and assessment;
- Eligibility for funding under the Title I and Title II sections of No Child Left Behind; and

- Affordable professional development—save when you schedule consecutive-day workshops.

University Credit—Correspondence Courses

AIMS offers correspondence courses through a partnership with Fresno Pacific University.

- Convenient distance-learning courses—you study at your own pace and schedule. No computer or Internet access required!

The tuition for each three-semester unit graduate-level course is $264 plus a materials fee.

The AIMS Instructional Leadership Program

This is an AIMS staff-development program seeking to prepare facilitators for leadership roles in science/math education in their home districts or regions. Upon successful completion of the program, trained facilitators become members of the AIMS Instructional Leadership Network, qualified to conduct AIMS workshops, teach AIMS in-service courses for college credit, and serve as AIMS consultants. Intensive training is provided in mathematics, science, process and thinking skills, workshop management, and other relevant topics.

Introducing AIMS Science Core Curriculum

Developed to meet 100% of your state's standards, AIMS' Science Core Curriculum gives students the opportunity to build content knowledge, thinking skills, and fundamental science processes.

- *Each* grade specific module has been developed to extend the AIMS approach to full-year science programs.
- *Each* standards-based module includes math, reading, hands-on investigations, and assessments.

Like all AIMS resources, these core modules are able to serve students at all stages of readiness, making these a great value across the grades served in your school.

For current information regarding the programs described above, please complete the following form and mail it to: P.O. Box 8120, Fresno, CA 93747.

Information Request

Please send current information on the items checked:

____ *Basic Information Packet* on AIMS materials ____ Hosting information for AIMS workshops
____ *AIMS Instructional Leadership Program* ____ AIMS Science Core Curriculum

Name _____ Phone _____

Address_____
      Street   City   State   Zip

Magazine

YOUR K-9 MATH AND SCIENCE CLASSROOM ACTIVITIES RESOURCE

The AIMS Magazine is your source for standards-based, hands-on math and science investigations. Each issue is filled with teacher-friendly, ready-to-use activities that engage students in meaningful learning.

- *Four issues each year (fall, winter, spring, and summer).*

Current issue is shipped with all past issues within that volume.

1820	Volume XX	2005-2006	$19.95
1821	Volume XXI	2006-2007	$19.95
1822	Volume XXII	2007-2008	$19.95

Two-Volume Combination

| M20507 | Volumes XX & XXI | 2005-2007 | $34.95 |
| M20608 | Volumes XXI & XXII | 2006-2008 | $34.95 |

Back Volumes Available
Complete volumes available for purchase:

1802	Volume II	1987-1988	$19.95
1804	Volume IV	1989-1990	$19.95
1805	Volume V	1990-1991	$19.95
1807	Volume VII	1992-1993	$19.95
1808	Volume VIII	1993-1994	$19.95
1809	Volume IX	1994-1995	$19.95
1810	Volume X	1995-1996	$19.95
1811	Volume XI	1996-1997	$19.95
1812	Volume XII	1997-1998	$19.95
1813	Volume XIII	1998-1999	$19.95
1814	Volume XIV	1999-2000	$19.95
1815	Volume XV	2000-2001	$19.95
1816	Volume XVI	2001-2002	$19.95
1817	Volume XVII	2002-2003	$19.95
1818	Volume XVIII	2003-2004	$19.95
1819	Volume XIX	2004-2005	$35.00

Volumes II to XIX include 10 issues.

Call 1.888.733.2467 or go to www.aimsedu.org

Subscribe to the AIMS Magazine

$19.95 a year!

AIMS Magazine is published four times a year.

Subscriptions ordered at any time will receive all the issues for that year.

AIMS Online—www.aimsedu.org

To see all that AIMS has to offer, check us out on the Internet at www.aimsedu.org. At our website you can search our activities database; preview and purchase individual AIMS activities; learn about core curriculum, college courses, and workshops; buy manipulatives and other classroom resources; and download free resources including articles, puzzles, and sample AIMS activities.

AIMS News
While visiting the AIMS website, sign up for AIMS News, our FREE e-mail newsletter. You'll get the latest information on what's new at AIMS including:

- New publications;
- New core curriculum modules; and
- New materials.

Sign up today!

AIMS Program Publications

Actions with Fractions, 4-9
Awesome Addition and Super Subtraction, 2-3
Bats Incredible! 2-4
Brick Layers II, 4-9
Chemistry Matters, 4-7
Counting on Coins, K-2
Cycles of Knowing and Growing, 1-3
Crazy about Cotton, 3-7
Critters, 2-5
Electrical Connections, 4-9
Exploring Environments, K-6
Fabulous Fractions, 3-6
Fall into Math and Science, K-1
Field Detectives, 3-6
Finding Your Bearings, 4-9
Floaters and Sinkers, 5-9
From Head to Toe, 5-9
Fun with Foods, 5-9
Glide into Winter with Math and Science, K-1
Gravity Rules! 5-12
Hardhatting in a Geo-World, 3-5
It's About Time, K-2
It Must Be A Bird, Pre-K-2
Jaw Breakers and Heart Thumpers, 3-5
Looking at Geometry, 6-9
Looking at Lines, 6-9
Machine Shop, 5-9
Magnificent Microworld Adventures, 5-9
Marvelous Multiplication and Dazzling Division, 4-5
Math + Science, A Solution, 5-9
Mostly Magnets, 2-8
Movie Math Mania, 6-9
Multiplication the Algebra Way, 6-8
Off the Wall Science, 3-9
Out of This World, 4-8
Paper Square Geometry:
    The Mathematics of Origami, 5-12
Puzzle Play, 4-8
Pieces and Patterns, 5-9
Popping With Power, 3-5
Positive vs. Negative, 6-9
Primarily Bears, K-6
Primarily Earth, K-3
Primarily Physics, K-3
Primarily Plants, K-3

Problem Solving: Just for the Fun of It! 4-9
Problem Solving: Just for the Fun of It! Book Two, 4-9
Proportional Reasoning, 6-9
Ray's Reflections, 4-8
Sense-Able Science, K-1
Soap Films and Bubbles, 4-9
Solve It! K-1: Problem-Solving Strategies, K-1
Solve It! 2nd: Problem-Solving Strategies, 2
Solve It! 3rd: Problem-Solving Strategies, 3
Solve It! 4th: Problem-Solving Strategies, 4
Solve It! 5th: Problem-Solving Strategies, 5
Spatial Visualization, 4-9
Spills and Ripples, 5-12
Spring into Math and Science, K-1
The Amazing Circle, 4-9
The Budding Botanist, 3-6
The Sky's the Limit, 5-9
Through the Eyes of the Explorers, 5-9
Under Construction, K-2
Water Precious Water, 2-6
Weather Sense: Temperature, Air Pressure, and Wind, 4-5
Weather Sense: Moisture, 4-5
Winter Wonders, K-2

Spanish Supplements*
Fall Into Math and Science, K-1
Glide Into Winter with Math and Science, K-1
Mostly Magnets, 2-8
Pieces and Patterns, 5-9
Primarily Bears, K-6
Primarily Physics, K-3
Sense-Able Science, K-1
Spring Into Math and Science, K-1

* Spanish supplements are only available as downloads from the
    AIMS website. The supplements contain only the student pages
    in Spanish; you will need the English version of the book for the
    teacher's text.

Spanish Edition
Constructores II: Ingeniería Creativa Con Construcciones
    LEGO® 4-9
    The entire book is written in Spanish. English pages not included.

Other Publications
Historical Connections in Mathematics, Vol. I, 5-9
Historical Connections in Mathematics, Vol. II, 5-9
Historical Connections in Mathematics, Vol. III, 5-9
Mathematicians are People, Too
Mathematicians are People, Too, Vol. II
What's Next, Volume 1, 4-12
What's Next, Volume 2, 4-12
What's Next, Volume 3, 4-12

For further information write to:
AIMS Education Foundation • P.O. Box 8120 • Fresno, California 93747-8120
www.aimsedu.org • 559.255.6396 (fax) • 888.733.2467 (toll free)

Duplication Rights

Standard Duplication Rights

Purchasers of AIMS activities (individually or in books and magazines) may make up to 200 copies of any portion of the purchased activities, provided these copies will be used for educational purposes and only at one school site.

Workshop or conference presenters may make one copy of a purchased activity for each participant, with a limit of five activities per workshop or conference session.

Standard duplication rights apply to activities received at workshops, free sample activities provided by AIMS, and activities received by conference participants.

All copies must bear the AIMS Education Foundation copyright information.

Unlimited Duplication Rights

To ensure compliance with copyright regulations, AIMS users may upgrade from standard to unlimited duplication rights. Such rights permit unlimited duplication of purchased activities (including revisions) for use at a given school site.

Activities received at workshops are eligible for upgrade from standard to unlimited duplication rights.

Free sample activities and activities received as a conference participant are not eligible for upgrade from standard to unlimited duplication rights.

Upgrade Fees

The fees for upgrading from standard to unlimited duplication rights are:
* $5 per activity per site,
* $25 per book per site, and
* $10 per magazine issue per site.

The cost of upgrading is shown in the following examples:
*   activity: 5 activities x 5 sites x $5 = $125
*   book: 10 books x 5 sites x $25 = $1250
*   magazine issue: 1 issue x 5 sites x $10 = $50

Purchasing Unlimited Duplication Rights

To purchase unlimited duplication rights, please provide us the following:
1. The name of the individual responsible for coordinating the purchase of duplication rights.
2. The title of each book, activity, and magazine issue to be covered.
3. The number of school sites and name of each site for which rights are being purchased.
4. Payment (check, purchase order, credit card)

Requested duplication rights are automatically authorized with payment. The individual responsible for coordinating the purchase of duplication rights will be sent a certificate verifying the purchase.

Internet Use

Permission to make AIMS activities available on the Internet is determined on a case-by-case basis.

• P. O. Box 8120, Fresno, CA 93747-8120 •
• permissions@aimsedu.org • www.aimsedu.org •
• 559.255.6396 (fax) • 888.733.2467 (toll free) •